PRAISE FOR *INTENTIONAL FAITH*

"Pastor Allen Jackson is a true example to me of faithfulness and humility, so I'm delighted he's written this book drawing on his real wisdom on how to effect meaningful spiritual change in our lives. Faith without action is no real faith; this book is a warm invitation to the real thing."

—**Eric Metaxas**, #1 New York Times bestselling author of
Bonhoeffer, *Martin Luther*, and *Miracles*; and host of the
nationally syndicated *Eric Metaxas Radio Show*

"When I think of a 'strong and steady' kind of faith, not easily quenched by fear, I think of the faith of men like Allen Jackson. If you've always wanted a wise mentor to disciple you in your spiritual journey, a personal Gandolf of sorts, to help guide you through the wilderness of life's challenges, you've found him. And in this book he's going to share his ancient secrets with you. Get ready for your faith to become more intentional, more real, and more solid."

—**Kirk Cameron,** actor and filmmaker best known for *Growing Pains*
and #1 grossing inspirational film of 2008, *Fireproof*

"Allen Jackson is a rare megachurch pastor in that he is a humble man with a true servant's heart. He doesn't put a spotlight on himself or his ministry but on Christ. The World Outreach Church he pastors is properly named for what it does, which is to touch the world through its myriad of ministries and missions around the globe. In his new book, *Intentional Faith*, he takes the reader on a challenging journey to align one's life with the Word of God. When some pastors are trying to be popular or 'relevant,' Allen Jackson focuses on sticking to the Scripture and living a life that doesn't escape challenges but powers through them. If you want to move from 'occasional' to 'intentional' in your Christian walk, this book will be a guide to get there!"

—**Mike Huckabee,** former governor of Arkansas, 2008 presidential
candidate, *New York Times* bestselling author, and host of
Huckabee

"Traditional thinking is that animals only learn by two methods—trauma and repetition—and more than likely a little of both. I sometimes think that the same is true of mankind. We have to get our fingers burned and learn the same lessons over and over again before they finally stick. From his experience and observation, Pastor Allen Jackson has written a book dealing with our desire to have a closer personal relationship with our Creator. *Intentional Faith* is about the common problems of self-doubt, forgiveness, and the desire to walk closer to God, written in everyday terminology and cut-to-the-chase conclusions."

　　—Charlie Daniels, American singer, songwriter, and
　　multi-instrumentalist best known for his #1 country
　　hit song "The Devil Went Down to Georgia"

"In Allen Jackson's *Intentional Faith*, you will receive Godly wisdom on how to grow in your faith in the Lord; therefore, you will create an environment in your home, your health, your business, and your relationships that allows God to work through you more efficiently and more noticeably. We all want God to give us things we want, but all too often we are too lazy and/or unintentional about doing what we should to see those things materialize. Faith is not like asking Santa Claus for a Christmas gift just one time and it magically showing up under the tree. Although we can't earn God's love and blessings, we can boldly ask for and welcome them by praying more, reading the Bible more, and loving and forgiving others more. In other words, we stand a better chance of receiving them by having an 'intentional faith.'"

　　—Josh Turner, actor, songwriter, and American country and gospel
　　singer best known for songs "Long Black Train" and "Your Man"

"What can you hope to become in one hundred days? Here are themes drawn from a lifetime of experience that have led to significant life changes in thousands of people. *Intentional Faith* unlocks the understandings a follower of Jesus Christ has found helpful in pursuing a life that would please God. Having walked alongside Allen Jackson for more than twenty years, I have observed him consistently practice what he describes in this book. He is as deliberate and intentional a leader as anyone I have known. The spotlight he puts on these areas for development carry a method and a promise. He has majored in approaching life changes in discrete and manageable bites. He would have all those who follow his path to experience a life of spiritual fruitfulness.

I have found his advice to be profoundly practical. Allen does not forcefully urge or seek to persuade in a dramatic fashion as do some presenters, but suggests simple, small steps that lead to perceptible progress. The results can be seen in terms of peace of mind and heart, and a growing confidence that God is aware and will assist where needed. Wherever you find yourself, Allen assures you can move toward an even better place, gradually and certainly. I am confident that anyone who walks in his guidance for the suggested one hundred days will be able to share their own convincing story of growth."

—**Carl George,** author and church growth consultant, Greenville, South Carolina

INTENTIONAL
FAITH

INTENTIONAL
FAITH

Aligning Your Life
with the
Heart of God

ALLEN JACKSON

NELSON
BOOKS

An Imprint of Thomas Nelson

385 2185

Published in Nashville, Tennessee, by Nelson Books, an imprint of Thomas
Nelson. Nelson Books and Thomas Nelson are registered trademarks of
HarperCollins Christian Publishing, Inc.

Published in association with Yates & Yates, www.yates2.com.

Thomas Nelson titles may be purchased in bulk for educational, business,
fund-raising, or sales promotional use. For information, please e-mail
SpecialMarkets@ThomasNelson.com.

Unless otherwise noted, Scripture quotations are taken from the Holy
Bible, New International Version®, NIV®. Copyright © 1973, 1978, 1984,
2011 by Biblica, Inc.® Used by permission of Zondervan. All rights reserved
worldwide. www.Zondervan.com. The "NIV" and "New International
Version" are trademarks registered in the United States Patent and
Trademark Office by Biblica, Inc.®

Scripture quotations marked KJV are from the King James Version. Public
domain.

Library of Congress Cataloging-in-Publication Data

Names: Jackson, Allen, 1958- author.
Title: Intentional faith: aligning your life with the heart of God / Allen
Jackson.
Description: Nashville: Thomas Nelson, 2020. | Includes bibliographical
references. | Summary: "Megachurch pastor Allen Jackson invites readers
on a 100-day adventure of experiencing God through ten biblical practices
that will reignite their faith and transform their lives"—Provided by
publisher.
Identifiers: LCCN 2019034589 (print) | LCCN 2019034590 (ebook) |
ISBN 9781400217250 (paperback) | ISBN 9781400217267 (ebook)
Subjects: LCSH: Faith. | Spiritual life—Christianity. | Christian life.
Classification: LCC BV4637 .J33 2020 (print) | LCC BV4637 (ebook) |
DDC 248.4/6—dc23
LC record available at https://lccn.loc.gov/2019034589
LC ebook record available at https://lccn.loc.gov/2019034590

Printed in the United States of America

20 21 22 23 24 LSC 10 9 8 7 6 5 4 3 2 1

*To the dedicated prayer warriors of
our world the difference makers.*

*Disciplined intercessors open doors of possibility for us
all. They often rise early or pray through the night.*

God responds to those who seek him.

CONTENTS

CONTENTS

PART FOUR
INTENTIONAL FAITH: GAINING SPIRITUAL HEALTH

PART FIVE
INTENTIONAL FAITH: AN INVITATION
TO KINGDOM IMPACT

INTRODUCTION

Between the following two ideas is where the reality of my existence is worked out:

Life is harder than I would prefer.
God is good.

If your season of life is more difficult than you anticipated, or if your faith feels stagnant and the joy of knowing God seems distant, do not stop believing the vibrant relationship with God you've imagined can be a reality.

Over the years, I've observed some characteristics in the lives of people who have deep, meaningful faith. I've studied and done my best to imitate those characteristics, to practice the ways of faith modeled for me. In this book, I share ten of these simple, lifesaving characteristics that open our lives to God's best. These fundamental building blocks align us with the heart of God.

Prepare yourself. In this book, you'll read stories of

those who've applied these same practices to their own lives and of the outcomes they've experienced. Then, at the end of this book, I'll invite you to join me in a one-hundred-day season of faith. It will be a journey of intentionally seeking alignment with the Creator of all things through applying these practices. As you enter that one-hundred-day season, I encourage you to journal your own experiences and God stories. Why? Because they'll no doubt be an encouragement to you as you look back, years in the future.

I pray this book will help you to seek God with intentionality, and that such intentional seeking will bring the clarity of God's direction. I pray the Holy Spirit will personally lead you into deep relationship with him as you go. I pray you'll find the life that God rewards, one of truth, freedom, and victory. Finally, I pray God strengthens you, and gives you the courage to press on toward the goal to win the prize for which God has called you heavenward in Christ Jesus (Phil. 3:14).

God is waiting for you to respond to him into the adventure of faith. Let's go.

PART ONE

INTENTIONAL FAITH: WHAT IS IT?

I press on toward the goal to win the prize for which God has called me heavenward in Christ Jesus.

—Philippians 3:14

Too often persons of faith have a passive outlook about God. They think, *If God wants me to do something, he will show me.* But the Bible describes a different posture. It tells us God is the rewarder of those who diligently seek him (Heb. 11:6). I don't know about you, but if the Creator of heaven and earth is dispensing rewards, I'm getting in line.

Let's explore together the attitudes and actions that result in God's involvement with us.

ONE

THE PROBLEM AND
THE PROMISE

My dad was a veterinarian, the kind who had a soft spot for even the most overlooked animals. Our home was a sort of rescue mission for the odd ducks, the castaways. He once brought home a blind lamb because the owner had no use for it. For a short season, he brought a de-scented skunk into our family, and when guests came to visit, we'd turn it loose and let it wander down the hall into the living room. It was a go-to prank that was always good for a shock and a laugh.

My dad's compassion was only outdone by his skill in treating those animals. There were afternoons he made house calls to help a family pet or went to the racetrack to treat a lame thoroughbred. There were times he was called to check on a litter of pups. And on occasion, he was called to a more complicated job. He would often take me along with him.

When I was thirteen years old, my dad took a call just before sunset. We then headed to a neighbor's farm, where a cow had been in labor for two days. She needed help, or the farmer could lose his cow and the calf. I'd helped my dad in similar situations, so I knew the drill. We knelt in the cold mud of our neighbor's field, the light of the pickup truck shining on us, and we tended to the animal. It took hours of gentle, quiet work. My dad first helped the cow relax, then he manipulated the calf in the womb to get it into position, and, over the span of an hour or more, he delivered a stillborn calf. A heaviness hung over that field, but a relief too; the cow would make it. She'd live to bear another calf another day.

Sincerity Isn't Enough

When outcomes matter, being sincere about achieving them is not sufficient. Too often Christians confuse enthusiasm with preparation. My dad sincerely loved animals, but that wasn't what saved the cow's life that day. Without knowledge and expertise, he likely wouldn't have achieved it. Without training, he'd have been unsuccessful.

Consider it: What if my dad had never read his textbooks, attended his classes, or studied for his exams? What if he hadn't spent time talking with his professors or learning from skilled veterinarians? What if he hadn't put his desire and passion into action? Would he have been able to help the animals he loved? Probably not. My dad's desire to save animals formed his intent, and *authentic intent is expressed with action.* He did whatever it took to become the best veterinarian. By expressing his intent through action, he was able to achieve the outcomes he wanted: helping the animals he loved so much.

We all want better life outcomes—better jobs, improved relationships, healthier bodies, greater emotional and spiritual health, and so on. We want richer, fuller lives. But just like most good things in life, these outcomes have long lead times. Well-adjusted children are not the result of a few casual moments of interaction. A beautiful garden of vegetables and fruits does not emerge from a quick response to a hunger pang. A thriving church is made up of believers who have committed to deepening their faith over the course of many years. Good things take cultivation. Good things take intention.

Intent is a powerful thing. It comes from deep within our spirit and soul. It's an expression of our will, our desires, and our emotions. Intent motivates us to action. It moves us toward the things we want. Have you considered its power, especially as it relates to your spiritual life?

So many of us want more from our relationship with God. So many of us want to see him actively working in our lives. But to achieve that outcome, we have to take incremental steps toward creating a deeper connection with him. It requires more than casually attending a few worship services or volunteering for the occasional service project. We must engage in certain intentional responses and cultivate God-oriented attitudes in order to experience the relationship God wants to have with us.

Here's the good news: You can develop the real and vibrant connection with God that you may have begun to doubt is possible. You can achieve the spiritually signifi-cant and fulfilling life you so desperately need. The change begins with the right intent expressed in action. What is that intent? In the first gospel of the Bible, Matthew recorded these words of Jesus:

> "So do not worry, saying, 'What shall we eat?' or 'What shall we drink?' or 'What shall we wear?' For the pagans run after all these things, and your heav-enly Father knows that you need them. But seek first his kingdom and his righteousness, and all these things will be given to you as well." (Matt. 6:31–33)

Jesus left no doubt. If we desire to know God, if we express that desire by seeking him above all else, we will find the full life.

But how do we seek him? We need a plan, some encour-agement, a little accountability, and a good reason. That's the purpose of this book.

Not a Cosmic To-Do List

Over the years—both before and after I was a pastor—I studied the lives of people who loved and served the Lord. People who followed him and had cultivated godly, peaceful lives. People who lived spiritually vibrant lives. Each had their own unique gifts, special talents and callings, and different ways of expressing their relationship with God. Yet there was symmetry in the way they lived their lives. There were common denominators in their daily practices.

I found that God rewards the simple expressions of intentional faith. I have not discovered something "new and improved." On the contrary, these practices have been in evidence across generations, since the first-century origins of the church. Here we are, the twenty-first-century edition of the book of Acts, and, like the early church, we must make choices to align ourselves with God's purposes. The invitation to one hundred days of faith will help us do just that. During this purposeful season of spiritual growth, I'll ask you to:

1. Intend to grow.
2. Intend to read the New Testament.
3. Intend to pray.
4. Intend to honor God in your home.
5. Intend to work with integrity.
6. Intend to teach the younger generation.

7. Intend to practice forgiveness.
8. Intend to welcome the Holy Spirit.
9. Intend to cultivate generosity.
10. Intend to finish well.

God's design has not changed from the very beginning, and neither have the practices for connecting with him. He's longed to connect with us through simple means. If you've been a follower of Christ for more than ten minutes, you probably know how important it is to read your Bible and pray. Deep down, you also know you ought to honor God in your home, work with integrity, and teach the younger generation about God. Even unbelievers know the importance of forgiveness and generosity. And could any follower of Christ argue that cooperation with the Holy Spirit isn't an imperative?

Even so, too many people of faith treat God as an item on a to-do list. Another responsibility to be checked off before pursuing what we "really want." I don't want to create another list of self-righteous dos and don'ts that add to the already ample load of guilt and shame that life often brings. Missing a day of reading your Bible will not ruin your spiritual well-being any more than missing a day of vegetables will ruin your physical health. At the same time, attention to a healthy diet—spiritual and physical—contributes to a happier, more productive life. The choices before us are not determined by our past God-experiences; the real issue is rooted in this moment. How can I cooperate with God right now, in the midst of my day?

God is actively looking for people who seek him, and he will respond to your sincere efforts. As you begin to have meaningful dialogue with God, you will see him more frequently in the world around you. You'll be less influenced by the circumstances of your everyday life, and instead, you'll be filled with more joy than you could have imagined. You'll experience a new perspective in your relationships— with your spouse, children, friends, and coworkers. You'll find yourself growing in wisdom, too, and that wisdom will lead to better life outcomes. How do I know? I've seen it time and time again. Both in my own life and in the lives of those I serve at my church.

Maybe all this sounds too good to be true. Maybe it sounds too simplistic or unsophisticated. Maybe you don't think it'll work for you. Or maybe you don't think it's doable. That's fine. I don't promise that this book will fix everything that ails you. Instead, see it as a doorway to a fuller, richer life of faith and spiritual connection.

Before we continue to the next chapter, let's pray.

A PRAYER FOR EXPRESSED INTENTION

Heavenly Father, I ask that you would give me the spirit of wisdom and revelation that I may know you better. I pray also that the eyes of my heart may be enlightened in order that I may know the hope to which you have called me, the riches of your glorious inheritance in the saints, and your great power expressed for me. I pray you would give me the grace to express my intent in action as I read this book. In Jesus' name, amen.

TWO

AN INVITATION TO INCREMENTAL CHANGE

I'd gathered with a group of mostly medical professionals for a home Bible study group. But before we dove in to the study for the night, a surgeon shared a recent experience.

Making his post-op rounds a few weeks before, he'd stopped at the nurse's station to take a few notes, when a young man approached him. Stopping in front of the surgeon, the young man pardoned himself, then asked for a favor. "You operated successfully on my mother years ago," he said, "and she's right over here, in the neighboring room. Would you mind stepping in and saying hello to her? She'd like to thank you in person." The surgeon agreed, not thinking twice about it, not knowing that he was about to have a kind of God-encounter. When he walked into the room, he saw a woman sitting up straight in a hospital bed. When they made eye contact, he recognized her immediately, even though he'd operated on thousands of patients. Even though her hair was now gray, and she was twenty years older than the last time he had seen her. She'd been an unforgettable patient.

He shared the woman's story with the group. She'd been rushed into the emergency room all those years ago with a serious stab wound in her chest. The point of the blade had pierced her ribs and gone directly into her heart. Remarkably, she had survived to arrive at the ER, and he spent tedious hours on the complicated surgery. When it was over, he'd left the operating room confident about her prospects. The woman recovered and left the hospital, as thousands of his patients had done over the years. But now she was back in that hospital bed, and she wanted to share a story with him.

She asked if he remembered her. He smiled and said he could never forget a surgery like that. When he asked how she was doing (despite the fact that she was in the hospital), she recounted the last twenty years of her life, and told him about how good it had been and how everything would have been so much different if he had not operated on her. And then she said something that caught him off guard: "I remember watching you perform the surgery on my heart."

He stood in silence for a moment before responding. He told her it was impossible, that her eyes were taped shut for the surgery.

She knew what she saw, she said. She'd watched as he repaired her heart. She then described various parts of the surgery in precise detail. It didn't hurt, she said. In fact, it'd been an amazing experience to see a surgeon employing his expertise, his craft.

It was an unsettling moment, and a bit awkward. No one in the history of his career had ever told him something like this. But after hearing her detailed account of the entire operation, he believed her.

"Why didn't you tell me this all those years ago?" he asked, but as soon as he asked her, he knew the reason. If she had told him she watched him perform *her* heart surgery while she was unconscious and her eyes were taped shut, he would have thought she was crazy. But there in that hospital room, he came to see that he'd become a different person over the years. Back then, he'd been a rock-star surgeon, an important man who enjoyed high-pressure situations and his ability to thrive under stress. He loved the ever-increasing paycheck he brought home. He was enamored by success, not just at work but also in his chosen hobby, where he trained field dogs for competition and had won national championships. But although he had plenty going for him, his personal life was deteriorating tragically. He saw his family as an intrusion, a tedious detail to be managed; he was disconnected from his wife and his kids. His friendship circles were shallow. And his spiritual walk was nonexistent.

He told our group that even though he'd grown up in church, and his family was part of a simple, country Pentecostal congregation, he couldn't wait to get away from the rules and regulations of that rural religious life. He wanted to make a different kind of life, where he was in control, so he put Jesus on the shelf and climbed the ladder of success all the way to the top. What he found at the pinnacle was underwhelming, though. Disappointing, even.

He shared the truth with us: if that woman sitting in the hospital bed had shared her story twenty years earlier, he would have had little interest. He wasn't ready for any kind of supernatural encounter in those days. He wasn't ready to see God's work in his everyday life.

He shared a larger truth too. Months before this experience, his wife told him, "There has to be something more than attending religious services with no expectation of change week after week." She then went to find a church where there was "some life and hope." She quietly slipped into our congregation without attracting any attention. She told him she was enamored by the people who seemed happy to be together. She never asked her husband to join her; she enjoyed the anonymity. After seeing the change in his wife, though, he told her, "I want to go with you."

He said something had changed in his life, which allowed him to receive his former patient's story: he had begun to welcome God into his life again. That shift changed everything, he said. But it wasn't overnight; the facade of his life was well crafted. The reality needed the power of God to write a new ending. Day-to-day problems didn't go away; there were still sick children, career challenges, and disappointments. But the grace of God had begun to touch his life, like a gentle breeze of hope. His heart turned toward his family, and he saw their value. An awareness of people as more than patients brought changes to his medical practice as well.

He'd spent decades pursuing his own interests and the outcomes had not satisfied. So the big surprise was that in yielding to Jesus, he found fulfillment. His home changed, his business expanded, and a future of hope emerged.

How Intentional Faith Leads to a Life-Changing Encounter with God

Changed intent changes you. And when you express your intent to cultivate a more meaningful connection with God, those changes will begin to emerge within you. God presents invitations to us; we choose our response.

As we move into this book, we'll look at the Gospels and see how those who encountered Jesus were forever changed. Jesus' public ministry began by the shores of a lake in Galilee when he moved from Nazareth to Capernaum. Nazareth is hidden away in the hills of Galilee, a small, isolated village. Capernaum was located on the King's Highway, an artery of transportation in the ancient world, and near the largest freshwater source in the region. It was a Jewish fishing village, uniquely equipped to facilitate crowds of people.

Jesus' ministry in Galilee was centered on a simple proposition: believe in me.

> What Jesus did here in Cana of Galilee was the first of the signs through which he revealed his glory; and *his disciples believed in him.* (John 2:11, emphasis mine)

Jesus demonstrated another way to interact with the world. He spoke with authority to unclean spirits and people were set free. The wind and the waves responded to his commands. He walked across a lake and invited his disciple to join him in the wonder. Sickness and disease yielded to his directions; even death released its hold when Jesus prayed. Those who chose to follow and learn from him were forever changed, and they became better fishermen.

> When he had finished speaking, he said to Simon, "Put out into deep water, and let down the nets for a catch."
>
> Simon answered, "Master, we've worked hard all night and haven't caught anything. But because you say so, I will let down the nets."
>
> When they had done so, they caught such a large number of fish that their nets began to break. So they signaled their partners in the other boat to come and

help them, and they came and filled both boats so full that they began to sink.

When Simon Peter saw this, he fell at Jesus' knees and said, "Go away from me, Lord; I am a sinful man!" (Luke 5:4–8)

Their faith life was dramatically altered. They experienced something that brought a new hope. They had an imagination of a transforming faith, demonstrations of God's presence and power.

The seventy-two returned with joy and said, "Lord, even the demons submit to us in your name." (Luke 10:17)

Their encounter with Jesus did not diminish their lives. Quite the contrary. Their lives expanded in possibility, experience, and excitement. It is intriguing to note those who chose to follow and those who declined the invitation. Our intent really does matter.

A wealthy young man with a carefully crafted education and a promising future approached Jesus, wanting to know what he must do to inherit eternal life. Jesus invited the young man to follow him; Mark even tells us that Jesus "loved him" (Mark 10:21). But the young man felt the invitation did not merit his time and attention.

In contrast, when Jesus invited Mary Magdalene, whose

lifestyle did not reflect Jesus' teaching, to follow him, she found the courage to obey. As a result, she became an integral part of Jesus' earthly initiative.

God does not need our success, our degrees, or even our hard-earned life experiences. He asks us to simply follow, to yield to the Creator of all things. It is a paradox: in yielding, we gain strength and discover power to interact with our world in entirely new ways.

An Invitation to Incremental Change

When Jesus invites people to follow him, he doesn't forecast the outcomes nor guarantee change overnight. He doesn't promise that we'll stop cussing in traffic tomorrow and never do it again, or that we'll start being patient with our children and never lose our patience again. He doesn't promise that the Hugh Hefners of the world will become Billy Grahams overnight. He only promises that if we follow him by doing the next right thing, day by day, month by month, year by year, he will walk with us each step of the way, blessing us so that we experience a fuller life. And though it will not all come at once, as you follow Christ, incremental changes will come, and you'll notice the shift.

My surgeon friend told our group about the ways he expressed and carried out his intent through daily training. He told us how arrogant he'd been. How he used to tell the residents, "If you're a competent surgeon, you don't need prayer." But when all that arrogance almost cost him his family and his friends, when he'd almost lost himself, he turned to God. He began praying, reading the Scriptures, taking the next godly step. He began to attend church regularly and tithe. He committed to honoring his wife and leading his children. Though nothing changed overnight, everything changed over time, incrementally, just like it had for Peter, Paul, and the other followers of Christ.

Now? His family loves him, as they face life's challenges together. He's known as a kind and generous man; some might even say humble. His eyes are open to the spiritual world, and he recognizes the miracles happening around him, like the woman who watched him repair her lacerated heart. Now he prays with patients before surgery, and if he happens to forget, his team reminds him. They've seen his life change—his joy, his generosity—and it's changed so many of them as well.

I believe his patients see it too, even if they don't always say so. Why? Because he finally has a real intent to live a faithful life. And, as authentic intent usually happens, it is expressed with action. Those actions led to his incremental change and connected him to the heart of the living God, and he is made new.

As you prepare for your own one-hundred-day journey into a more intentional faith, expect to see a change in your life. And as you experience the power of this season, as you begin to see the changes just like my friend did, journal the progress. Months and years later, you'll look back and see how an incremental change led to the next incremental change, and how all those changes brought new momentum to your spiritual journey.

A PRAYER FOR INCREMENTAL CHANGE

Almighty God, you are my creator and my deliverer. I trust in you. Nothing is hidden from your awareness. No challenge is so great that you withdraw in fear. Help me to choose the pathways that bring your very best to my life. Give me an understanding heart and a listening ear that I might recognize your invitations. Grant me the courage to follow you and deliver me from evil. In Jesus' name, amen.

THREE

THE RESISTANCE AND
THE ASSURANCE

Big hat, no cattle," that's what my grandfather used to say about men who wanted to dress the part of cowboys without putting in the hard work of running cattle. And it's been my experience that much of Christianity is taught the same way. If you look the part, if you say the right things, if you show up at church looking the right way and praying the right prayers, that's enough. But this kind of all-appearance, no-substance Christianity won't get you through when the times are tough. And rest assured, times will get tough.

When I sat down to write this chapter, I was reminded of a day not too long ago when I officiated a funeral. Leah's upbringing had been rough, and her young adulthood, very difficult. Still, in her early thirties she'd come to follow

Jesus and had committed herself to the things of God. I'd watched as she matured spiritually, and her faith took off like a wheat stalk. I watched as she made peace with the world around her and became an encourager in the lives of others. She met a wonderful man whom she later married. It was the classic Cinderella story: girl endures the hardships of life, finds her Prince Charming, and proceeds to live happily ever after. Except for the last part.

Only a few months after the wedding, Leah visited the doctor and discovered she had inoperable brain cancer. Time was short; the end of her life and new marriage were near. She could have been angry with God, could have been bitter about the way her already difficult life was ending. She could have walked away from her faith, but she didn't. In fact, she never wavered. She stayed committed to the very end.

I'd had one of those hard days, the kind where I'd rather be anything but a pastor. Still, I said all the right things at the funeral. I spoke of how Leah had remained faithful, despite having had such a difficult life, despite having received such a terrible diagnosis. I was sure she was with her Savior, and I said as much. But it didn't make the loss any easier. To me it seemed Leah had been taken too soon. As I drove away from the funeral, I couldn't help myself, and I made my complaints known to God. Why Leah? She was too young, had struggled so much, had been so faithful, and had only just found the kind of peace and stability promised to those who live with intentional faith. If anyone deserved a miracle, hadn't it been Leah? And what about her new husband? Was it fair to him?

I went on, sharing my dissatisfaction with God. But suddenly, while I was waiting at a traffic light, I heard that still, small voice I'd learned to recognize over the years: *I know how to get my children home.*

It was the voice of the Holy Spirit speaking, silencing my complaints. I sat in that correction, listening, absorbing, understanding. And though God never broke the silence of my car, he spoke into my heart. I had a new perspective on Leah's life. She had faced many difficulties, but she had finished well. On the day she died, she was more ready than she'd ever been to enter eternity. Nothing had been stolen from her. In fact, she had received everything: peace, wholeness, and freedom.

I know how to get my children home, I heard again.

I continued to listen. As I did, I realized Leah had actually lived a life of faith, one aligned with God's heart. Though the benefits she received on earth were short-lived, she had an eternal reward that was secure. In that moment, the truth I knew became real: the life of intentional faith brings tangible results. That doesn't always mean we'll experience a life of ease and blessing, at least not on earth. We'll still experience death, loss, and grief. Things might sometimes seem unfair. And those things will undo us, if there's no substance to our faith.

The Most Significant Outcomes
Require Significant Intention

We all want certain life outcomes, some results. We might want better health, such as losing a few extra pounds or lowering our cholesterol level. We might want bigger careers, bigger assignments, bigger influences. We might want better-behaved children or a better marriage. We might want simple things, such as a bumper crop of summer tomatoes in the backyard. But in each of these areas, the outcomes won't come without intention and effort. Desire alone isn't enough in life; the same holds true in the spiritual life.

I wish I had a quick fix for spiritual growth, some miracle pill that will bring us into perfect alignment with the heart of God. But just like everything else in life, walking with God takes commitment to action. You have to engage in the thoughts and behaviors that lead to spiritual growth. You have to commit to those things no matter the season, whether good or bad. And the one-hundred-day invitation this book will walk you into is meant to help establish this kind of commitment.

Life is more difficult than we wish it were. But it can also be more amazing than we ever imagined. It's true that we won't always have the solutions to life's more difficult situations. We won't always be able to negotiate those perfect storms of life that seem to know our addresses. We'll always encounter roadblocks, big and small. But if we learn to align our lives with the heart of God, if we learn to hear from him and walk with him, we'll experience amazing outcomes. We'll experience the truth Jesus preached: "I have come that they may have life, and have it to the full" (John 10:10).

A PRAYER FOR STRENGTH AND COURAGE TO FOLLOW

Heavenly Father, I need your help. In my own strength and wisdom, I am inadequate for the challenges before me. Give me the courage to follow you. May I recognize the pathway to freedom and joy. Holy Spirit, direct my steps. Grant me a receptive heart that I may live in the freedom of the almighty God. In Jesus' name, amen.

PART TWO

INTENTIONAL FAITH: DAILY NOURISHMENT

Blessed is the one
*   who does not walk in step with the wicked*
or stand in the way that sinners take
*   or sit in the company of mockers,*
but whose delight is in the law of the LORD,
*   and who meditates on his law day and night.*
That person is like a tree planted by streams
*   of water,*
*   which yields its fruit in season*
and whose leaf does not wither—
*   whatever they do prospers.*

—Psalm 1:1–3

The God of the Bible is a personal God who responds to those who actively seek him. Even today, when we express an intentional faith in tangible, daily action, we encounter the Father from whom every good and perfect gift flows (James 1:17). But what kind of daily actions pave the way to this kind of divine encounter?

Success in any endeavor is linked to our attention to fundamentals. Our spiritual life is no different. You cannot hire someone to exercise to ensure your cardio fitness. Similarly, your spiritual well-being cannot be achieved by listening to a pastor. I would like to extend an invitation for you to set the following daily choices that hold the potential to bring real transformation:

- Pursue daily spiritual growth.
- Engage God in prayer.
- Read the Bible.

These daily actions may seem obvious, especially to those who have a religious background. Don't see them as burdensome additions to a daily list of responsibilities—they form the foundation of a relationship with the Creator of all things! The investment of a few minutes every day can truly help to open a new future. If you are comfortable with your status quo, you don't need to read further. But if you have an interest in a new future, an opportunity awaits.

FOUR

INTEND TO GROW

My dad's career as a veterinarian pulled up my childhood roots. At the age of nine, my brothers and I helped my parents pack all our worldly possessions in a truck and made our way from the beaches of sunny South Florida to the sweltering farm country of Murfreesboro, Tennessee. My dad's main attraction was the Tennessee Walking Horses, but my parents also wanted to rear their three sons in an environment that provided a slower pace and a better future.

I was too young to understand the full implications of the move. Had I understood that I'd be trading the beaches and thoroughbred tracks of sunny Florida for the stale humidity and overgrown pastures of Tennessee, I might have objected. But now I'm grateful for their decision.

We put down roots in Murfreesboro, and my dad began a small veterinary practice. Our home served as his base of operation, his clinic, and we all chipped in. My mom was the secretary. My bedroom was the drug storage room for a while. Our kitchen table occasionally served as a treatment space for someone's pet. I'd like to tell you they were the best of times, but the truth is, they were the toughest of times. I was in a new town, in a new school with no friends, and nothing much to look forward to. I was bumping into a life lesson that would be revisited in the years ahead: growth emerges from change.

Two years earlier, God had completely redirected our lives. My mom was diagnosed with cancer and given a two-year life expectancy. With a husband graduating from vet school and three young boys, a devastating illness was a formula for desperation. Although my family faithfully attended church, we were not Christians, except in name. On her way to the Mayo Clinic for a radical surgery, my mom prayed: "If there is a God, let me know the truth before I die." After three days of examinations, a doctor gave a report: "We cannot find the cancer. Go home and take care of your family."

Eight weeks later, as they were still reeling from the encounter with God's miraculous healing, a Methodist Sunday school teacher in Hollywood, Florida, told my parents they could be born again. They took the teacher up on the offer and, excited to understand another piece of the God equation, sought out Bible studies and groups of Christians throughout South Florida.

Two years removed from a life-altering miracle, in a

new state, with a new business, a friend prompted my parents to have a Bible study in our home, a step well beyond their comfort zone. They took the risk, though, and over time, that Bible study filled with all sorts of different people from our small community, one where it would have been easy to fall through the cracks of the religious system. The Bible study group was diverse, our version of the island of misfit toys. It was a group of people who recognized their need to know God in a more personal way—some because of desperate circumstances and some because God had begun to stir their hearts. During that time, I learned another principle of spiritual growth: God brings change using the least likely people if those people are committed to growth.

Over the years that followed, I watched God work in the lives of dozens of people. It was a curious parade of characters who crossed the threshold of that home Bible study. A woman rejected by her husband and disabled by lupus and a broken heart was restored. A young woman, alone and pregnant, found a path toward life and a better future. It seemed each week God would direct someone searching for hope onto the path of the group. In each case, there were the same outcomes. We learned the importance of our Bibles. We learned that prayer was necessary because we needed God's help. And we learned that overcoming challenges is a part of everyone's journey. As I watched, I discovered a third principle of growth: spiritual growth doesn't happen by accident. In order to grow spiritually, you have to intend to grow.

Wanting and Wishing Are Not Enough

I love many things about summertime in Tennessee, but among my favorites are summer vegetables: tomatoes, peppers, squash, zucchini, and cucumbers. There's just something special about the vegetables that grow in this part of the country. It's safe to say that every single year I would love to see a bumper crop of summer vegetables in my backyard. I would love to look out my kitchen window and see a bountiful harvest ready and waiting. But simply wanting and wishing won't make it so. Standing in front of my church and claiming a summer harvest won't bring in the fresh vegetables. Looking out the window and praying, "Jesus, send those tomatoes!" won't make it happen.

If I want Tennessee vegetables, I have to make a concerted effort. I have to till the ground, plant the seeds, water the garden, spray the squash, and stake up the tomatoes when they get too large to support themselves. And eventually, I'll have to pick the vegetables, wash them, and slice them if I want to enjoy the harvest.

What's true of growing vegetables is true of spiritual growth. We can't stand around, wanting and wishing and hoping we'll get results. And if we're doing things that inhibit spiritual growth, we can't continue with the status quo and expect different results. Instead, we have to do what it takes to grow spiritually by taking intentional, conscious action. Some of those actions might be weekly (faithfully participating in church), monthly (tithing), or even moment-by-moment (cooperating with the Holy Spirit). But before I explore these groups of practices in depth, let's concentrate on three *daily* practices on which the life of faith is built:

1. Intend to grow.
2. Intend to read the Bible.
3. Intend to pray.

I'll examine reading the Bible and praying in the next two chapters. But know this: you'll never engage in daily prayer and Bible study if you don't intend to grow spiritually. It's this intent that fuels and propels all other action. It animates and motivates us to take the necessary steps to become healthy spiritual beings.

Intending to Grow Spiritually Isn't About Religious Habit

While we're exploring the connection between intentional action and spiritual growth, remember that this intent to grow goes beyond participating in the dry certainty of religious habit. It goes beyond dressing up for Sunday services, or keeping yourself from cussing, or donating to your local church. Your intent to grow has to be a daily endeavor to understand, know, and align your life with the heart of God. Even if you've been walking with God for years, you have to keep pursuing daily growth. Even Paul, who had an extraordinary, blinding, voice-from-the-heavens encounter with God, wasn't content with this one-time experience. He pursued intentional growth for all the years after his conversion. In his letter to the Philippians, he wrote:

> Brothers and sisters, I do not consider myself yet to have taken hold of it. But one thing I do: Forgetting what is behind and straining toward what is ahead, I press on toward the goal to win the prize for which God has called me heavenward in Christ Jesus. (Phil. 3:13–14)

Paul understood the truth about spiritual growth. He'd had a personal revelation of Jesus. He was academically accomplished. He was a leader in the church and had led countless people to Christ. He wrote scores of letters, which comprise the majority of the New Testament. Still, he didn't think he'd arrived. He continued to pursue God with intention and dedication for the rest of his life. He intended to continue growing, no matter what he'd already achieved. What was the result? A fruitful, ongoing, eternal ministry that still impacts the world today.

Your impact might not be as big as Paul's or Billy Graham's or your local pastor's, but by expressing your intent to grow through directed actions, you can grow in spiritual maturity and connection with God. As you do, you'll experience the life outcomes God has for you—life outcomes that have a direct kingdom impact. I know, because I've experienced it.

Intentional Growth and Your Kingdom Impact

That home Bible study that started all those years ago continued to grow, because the individuals in it continued to grow. Never content with where they were spiritually, each member pursued God with great intention. And over time, the group grew so large, they couldn't continue meeting in my parents' home; they needed a larger meeting place, like a church building.

The little group that began through the prompting of my parents' friend gave birth to the congregation I now serve. And forty years later, I can see that our congregation was no accident. Today, with thousands of people and so many stories being shared day after day, it is tempting to say I knew what God was doing all along. I didn't, though. In fact, often, I felt like a failure. It felt like we were up against challenge after challenge. But after years of intentional faithfulness toward spiritual growth, we can see how God used the lives of ordinary people who were intent on growing their faith to shape the God-story of Middle Tennessee.

The principles gleaned in those early years in the home Bible study are still informing our lives. We still express our daily intention to grow spiritually. Though we're not perfect, our brokenness and failed attempts don't exclude us from the work. In fact, they just serve as proof that ordinary people can do extraordinary things when they invite God into the middle of it. They serve as proof that a band of misfit toys from Tennessee can have an impact that reaches to the uttermost parts of the earth.

As we learn to align our lives with the heart of God, let's start by intending to grow a little every day. And if you don't know where to start, that's okay. Ask God to show you the places in your life where you need spiritual maturity as you read this book. Ask him to help you grow in the expression of your intentional faith each day. As you do, as you walk in the practices and responses written in this book, notice how participating with God—how aligning your heart with his—leads to growth, and keep a note of those observations in your journal. And whatever you do, don't stop.

AN EXERCISE OF INTENT

1. Examine your life. What are some areas where you've desired growth and have pursued it with

intention? For example, have you pursued business growth? Fitness growth? The growth of your influence? Have you pursued growth in your marriage? What about spiritual growth?

2. List the godly people in your life who've pursued spiritual growth. What characteristics mark their lives?

3. Commit to asking God each day to show you the areas of your life where you need spiritual growth. And as you go about your day, take note of how he's growing you in those areas.

A PRAYER FOR BEGINNING A LIFE OF FAITH

Almighty God, I am a sinner. I need a Savior. Forgive me of my sins as I forgive those who have sinned against me. I believe Jesus is your Son, that he died on a cross for my sins, and that he was raised to life for my justification. I choose him as Lord of my life today, and I want to serve him with my whole heart. Amen.

FIVE

INTEND TO READ THE NEW TESTAMENT

orty days before her fortieth birthday, Jean made a commitment: she was going to read through the Bible before crossing into the next decade of her life. She figured reading the Scripture in its entirety would serve as sort of a milestone for her fortieth year, a marker; and as a stay-at-home mom whose youngest child was now in kindergarten, she finally had the time to accomplish the goal. At least, that's what she thought.

Of course, reading the Bible in forty days is an ambitious goal, perhaps too ambitious, which Jean soon discovered. But she didn't fall short because of poor planning or lack of willpower or the intrusion of daily to-dos. Instead, her best intentions were hijacked by some unexpected medical news. She hadn't been feeling well, so she scheduled a doctor's visit.

One visit gave way to the next, and on her fortieth birthday—the day she'd hoped to finish the last chapter of Revelation—she sat in the doctor's office and received the news: she had stage four breast cancer. She was told, even with aggressive chemotherapy, her life expectancy was only twenty months.

"I thought I was solid, but I wasn't," Jean later told me. "I was shaken." She knew God loved her, she said, but she wasn't sure whether he heard her or whether he still healed. And, as the questions came, she realized "just how shallow her faith was" (her words, not mine).

Jean began chemotherapy. As her energy waned, and she was relegated to the sidelines of her usually busy life, she began asking God to show up in her quiet, lonely moments. She turned to prayer, asking what God wanted from her in this tragic season. In that quiet moment, she recalled her promise to read the Bible through, a promise she'd forgotten in this season of sickness. Now, with a death sentence hanging over her and filled with an urgency to finish what she'd started, she opened the Scriptures to the book of John—the place she'd stopped reading—and read the words of Jesus:

"This sickness will not end in death. No, it is for God's glory so that God's Son may be glorified through it." (John 11:4)

There, in her living room, the Scriptures washed over her and filled her with hope, peace, and something like new energy. She ran up the stairs to her bedroom, found her husband, and told him, "I believe I have a word from the Lord." It was a word that came just when she needed it, just at the right time, and she and her husband clung to it. They did not abandon the doctors and their treatment, of course. But with this new promise from God, they were filled with hope.

Reading the Bible Before the Crisis

The Bible says that God loves us, and he wants to bless us with every spiritual blessing in Christ (Eph. 1:3). It's a line so many of us have heard before, but ask yourself: Would you know this truth without reading the Bible? How would you discover the spiritual blessings in Christ without reading the Bible, God's book of promised blessings?

Before we push any further into a discussion on the blessings God has for us, particularly those given through the Scriptures, let's pause to acknowledge the elephant in the room. Everyone who has even a marginal interest in Christianity knows reading the Bible is a good idea. We know the Bible is a powerful book, one that gives us guidance and instruction. But for the most part, we take Scripture in micro-doses when we attend church or perhaps when we read a brief devotional. We find ourselves lacking the motivation to read it as much as we should. And when we do sit down to read it, we move quickly over the hardest parts, because we find it confusing and distant from our daily responsibilities. For so many of us, reading the Bible is similar to eating healthier and exercising more—it's a good idea, but we don't always implement it into our life plan, at least, not until some life crisis comes along.

As a pastor, I walk with my congregants as they are confronted with the unexpected and the unwanted. A cancer diagnosis, like Jean's. A loss of a spouse or child. A divorce. And when these tragedies come knocking, what was once a vague notion—*I should read my Bible more*—becomes an imperative. I say this with no criticism or judgment. You'd better believe that if I were met with a cancer diagnosis, I'd read my Bible with much greater intention. And I'm a pastor! That said, I have a suggestion. Rather than wait for an uninvited life crisis to foster desperate biblical scholarship, let's invest a few minutes each day and adopt the practice of reading our Bibles as an expression of faith and discipline—a prerequisite for any disciple.

Committing ourselves to reading the Word of God pays both spiritual and tangible rewards. As he did with Jean, God has a remarkable track record of responding to those who seek him through the Scriptures, whether you're in a season of crisis or not. And you don't have to be burdened with understanding everything you read, nor do you have to have some great spiritual insight every time you read. If you simply submit your schedule and attention to the Bible for a few minutes each day, you'll discover an amazing principle: as you read the Bible, the Bible reads you.

The Power of Jesus' Story

Let's be candid, though. The Bible—God's Word—can be a daunting book, right? It is composed of sixty-six separate books and spans hundreds of pages. It contains historical narratives, poetry, prophetic warnings, personal letters, and apocalyptic literature. It's sometimes violent, sometimes suggestive, and the stories in it are often unbelievable. What's more, the narrative flow isn't always linear, and depending on the version you have, the language can be difficult to understand. The Bible can be a difficult read. But that difficulty can be navigated if you have a plan. If you accept the invitation to embark on a purposeful season of spiritual growth, follow the reading plan in the back of this book, starting with the Gospels, and finish the New Testament by the end of your one-hundred-day commitment.

The Gospels, the first four books of the New Testament—Matthew, Mark, Luke, and John—can be a great on-ramp. Jesus said, "Anyone who has seen me has seen the Father" (John 14:9). The Gospels present a narrative of Jesus' entry into human time and space. They show how God's Son took on an "earth suit" of human skin and walked among us, how he became a revelation of God's heart for us.

Through the words of the gospel writers, you'll be transported into the story. You'll fish on the lake of Galilee or stand in the cemetery with the awestruck group who witnessed Lazarus emerge from the tomb. I suspect you'll begin to empathize with the disciples as they struggled to understand Jesus' parables, make sense of his healing power, and keep up with his ideas and invitations. You'll feel the crush of the crucifixion, the joy of his resurrection, and the wonder of his ascension. You'll see how God loved us enough to come down from heaven, to be *with* us. You'll see how willing he was to give everything *for* us. And as you begin to see the truth of God's love as told through his story, you'll find that reading the Bible is not a burdensome intrusion that must be tolerated because of a misplaced sense of religious obligation. Instead, you'll find that opening your mind to God's thoughts and perspectives prepares you for a new way of living, of being. It prepares you for a new sort of existence.

As I Begin the Reading Plan, What Should I Know?

As you read the Gospels, know that each writer takes a unique approach, sharing different facets of Christ's teaching. Matthew was written for the Jewish audience of the day. It begins with a long genealogy, proving Jesus' bloodline connection to King David, before jumping into the birth story of Christ. It's a book that emphasizes the Jewishness of Jesus, and often finds Jesus pitted against the teachers of the religious law.

Mark, the shortest of the Gospels and believed to be the first written, steps over the birth narratives of Jesus and launches into his ministry. Mark writes as if he is in a hurry to get to the punch line. Consider the proclamation he shares in just the first chapter of his gospel:

> After John was put in prison, Jesus went into Galilee, proclaiming the good news of God. "The time has come," he said. "The kingdom of God has come near. Repent and believe the good news!" (Mark 1:14–15)

See how much ground he covers in the first fifteen verses. See how he announces the kingdom of God. Mark invites his readers to repent and to become disciples right along with the others Jesus recruited.

Luke, the author of the gospel that bears his name and the book of Acts, was a physician. He writes with both the keen eye of a diagnostician and a unique awareness of the presence and the power of the Spirit of God. Listen to how he frames Jesus' ministry: "Jesus returned to Galilee in the power of the Spirit, and news about him spread through the whole countryside" (Luke 4:14). As you read the gospel of Luke, you'll notice his viewpoint, how human limits cannot inhibit God's plans because the Spirit of God can overcome any human obstacle.

In the gospel of John, the language is a bit more straight-forward, but the story is more personal. John was the disciple closest to Jesus. He was the one who, years later, would be entrusted with the final book of the Bible: the book of Revelation. (In Revelation 1:1, John writes that it is "the rev-elation from Jesus Christ, which God gave him to show his servants what must soon take place.") More than the other Gospels, John invites readers to become a part of the entourage; he invites us into the secrets Christ shared with his inner circle.

As you read through the Gospels, take the journey with the writers as they follow Jesus. After all, isn't the story of Jesus worth the investment of a few minutes a day? And as you follow Jesus alongside Matthew, Mark, Luke, and John, notice how new ideas, new thoughts, and new strength begin to emerge, both in the moment and throughout the day, just like it did for Jean.

As Jean experienced, the Bible can meet you in your darkest hour of need and give you a word of hope to hold on to. It can give you direction when you're wrestling with a difficult life choice or provide colorful commentary in your moments of joy. It can cut through the average, mun-dane, day-to-day moments and speak something fresh and exciting to you. Why? Because the Bible, although delivered through human beings, is a revelation of the Creator of all things. It is a source of insight and understanding that's not limited by our own human frailty or intellectual abilities. It breathes hope and truth into the murkiness of a world of selfish ambition. It's a tool to help us cut away the negative thoughts, attitudes, and actions. The author of the book of Hebrews wrote as much, giving us a focused thesis of the value of God's Word:

> For the word of God is alive and active. Sharper than any double-edged sword, it penetrates even to dividing soul and spirit, joints and marrow; it judges the thoughts and attitudes of the heart. (Heb. 4:12)

If you're honest, you know how difficult it can be to know your own heart and sort through your own motives. We are all prone to do things we'd rather not do or desire things we'd rather not desire. Don't you struggle with your emotions and attitudes like I do? And when the outcomes really matter, we often need wisdom greater than our own. As the writer of Hebrews notes, God provides that wisdom for so many of our everyday problems if we'll just take hold of it. Where? In the pages of your Bible.

Consider, for example, the biblical teaching—Jesus' teaching, in fact—on anxiety, a common struggle throughout every age. In his first recorded sermon in the New Testament, Jesus addressed a crowd who'd gathered to hear him, preaching,

> "So do not worry, saying, 'What shall we eat?' or 'What shall we drink?' or 'What shall we wear?' For the pagans run after all these things, and your heavenly

Father knows that you need them. But seek first his kingdom and his righteousness, and all these things will be given to you as well." (Matt. 6:31–33)

Hear Jesus' teaching on anxiety, how he assures us that we don't need to worry! In fact, he makes the statement five times in the same chapter. Imagine a life liberated from the exhaustion of worry and anxiety. And why did Jesus preach on the topic? Because he knew just how prone to worry we all are. He knows what we need—rest from anxiety—and he'll provide it for us, so long as we seek the kingdom first. Through this dramatic reassignment of priority, anxiety will be sucked out of life. See how aligning our hearts with the truth of God's Word leads to better emotional and physical outcomes.

What's true of anxiety is true of a whole host of other issues. By reading the Gospels, we'll discover the power of peace-making and forgiveness. We'll come to understand Christ's teaching on work, compassion, and generosity. We'll come to understand how Jesus wants us to love each other, both those in our immediate social spheres and those on the margins of society. We'll see the power of trusting him in every facet of our lives.

Seeing Is Believing, and I'm a Believer

I've been a pastor now for over thirty-five years, and I've seen hundreds, maybe thousands, commit to the daily practice of reading the Bible. I've watched as they've allowed God's Word to soak into their lives and change them. I've heard story after story of God's Word speaking to people just when they needed it most, people like Jean.

I bet you're wondering, What ever happened to Jean? She's flourishing! And if you were to ask her today, she'd tell you her life changed the day God gave her the promise through his Word. Though she was given only twenty months to live, she's now made it more than four years, and she's continued to study God's Word ever since. God has proven his faithfulness not just to the passage he had given her but through so many other promises too. Now Jean swears by the power of God's Word, and how it brings peace, comfort, and direction to her daily life—all because she's committed to reading it regularly.

As you enter your one-hundred-day journey of faith, commit to reading the New Testament. It's a foundational practice for those who want to live the kind of life God rewards. And as you read, journal your insights. Record the ways Jesus meets you right where you are, and then lean on his promises. See the difference it makes in your life.

AN EXERCISE OF INTENT

1. When was the last time you read the Bible for a week straight without missing a single day? Have

you ever? If you commit to start reading daily, make a list to track your progress.

2. As you read, write in your journal any difficult passages. Write down questions you may have, or thoughts about the passages that might occur to you, then find a pastor or a friend to discuss them.

3. Make a list of the ways you might be able to engage in corporate reading of the Bible. Could you read a short passage of scripture each day with your family? Is there a coworker you can study the Bible with once a week? What about a friend? Make a plan to read the Bible with someone and stick with it. (See the daily reading plan in the back of this book.)

A PRAYER FOR GOD'S WORD TO SPEAK

Heavenly Father, I know your Word is sharper than any two-edged sword, that it cuts through the noise of this world. I know you communicate with me through the Scriptures, and you want me to learn and grow as I hear from you. Teach me through the reading of your Scripture. Help me to know you better through it and lead me into deeper intimacy with you. Holy Spirit, help me to learn. In Jesus' name, amen.

SIX

INTEND TO PRAY

Twelve of us—mostly doctors and dentists, all from the church—were headed for Peru for a medical mission trip. In less than a week, we were to load a boat and make our way down a tributary of the Amazon River, serving the people in more remote villages without access to health care. I was the token religious person, tagging along to carry supplies and provide some devotional support. Our work was simple: float downriver at night, tie up along the shore before dawn, set up medical and dental clinics, and serve the local population. We couldn't wait to get on Peruvian soil.

In the days before our scheduled departure, a small group of friends approached me after church. They'd been keeping up with the region we would be visiting and knew this wouldn't be the typical short-term mission trip. They said there was some political unrest in the area, the region

51

was remote, and communication would be difficult. So they agreed to meet each morning at 6:30 and pray for our little missionary band. I thanked them, happy to have interested friends who were willing to invest the time and effort to provide an hour of prayer each morning.

That very week, we set out for what can only be described as a life-changing trip. We spent days extending care to young and old, who emerged from the jungle. For those with no access to health care, having a tooth pulled, tending to a snake bite, or delivering a baby were life-altering events, and to have doctors and dentists with education and training made all the difference. As a result, villagers came from miles away to receive medical attention. Among them was a woman in labor, who arrived in a dugout canoe late one night. The next morning, after being helped through labor, she and the new baby climbed back into their canoe and disappeared around a bend in the river. It was a beautiful moment, the woman making her way back home holding a new life. As I watched her go, I was reminded of how easy and insulated our lives in Tennessee really were.

We returned home with changed hearts and new perspectives on the blessings in our lives. And within days of being back, we visited that little prayer group and shared our stories, noting how their prayers had impacted our lives. Someone in the group mentioned that another team was leaving for Kenya in a few days and asked if we should keep the prayer group going for another week or so. We decided it was a good idea, so they continued to meet each morning for prayer. This time for the Kenya team.

What started as a missions prayer team morphed into something more permanent. The group didn't stop praying when the team from Kenya returned. They kept meeting every morning, praying for the needs of the church, for the needs of one another, for the needs of our country, and beyond. It's been eighteen years since that trip to the Amazon, and the morning prayer team has not missed a single day. Seven days a week, 365 days a year, members of that group get together. Imagine it: eighteen years of uninterrupted prayer. And if you were to translate those prayers into changed lives, the number would be immeasurable.

The group doesn't have some fancy name. We simply call it Morning Prayer, and everyone in the church is invited. The number of participants varies by day. There are anywhere from fifteen to forty people who join in, but it's open to anyone who would like to attend. Some come for a season and just listen; others participate for a few weeks while walking through a difficult time. It has proven to be a training place for younger people to listen and learn to pray.

The God-stories that have emerged from these Morning Prayer meetings have changed our church. I've stopped saying they're remarkable, because truth be told, the stories simply display the character of God, who desires to be involved in our lives.

The Connected Life Is the Prayer-Filled Life

Alexander Graham Bell won the first patent for a telephone in 1876, a device that fundamentally changed the way we communicate. And for more than 125 years, the telephone was used for one reason: to make phone calls. In June 2007, though, that paradigm shifted when Apple released the first iPhone. The phone introduced us to the possibility of a multifaceted personal communication device. From phone calls to text messaging to social media to the way we consume entertainment, smartphones have become an integral part of how we manage our lives, operate our businesses, and entertain ourselves.

Similarly, many of us still use prayer for a particular purpose: to make our requests known to God in times of crisis. This reason for communicating with God isn't bad. But I want to invite you to imagine prayer in a new way: more as a way to process life *with* God, than as a way to talk *to* God in times of crisis.

Imagine prayer as less of an old rotary-dial landline phone and more of an iPhone—a personal communications tool. Prayer can become an expression of awareness that God is alive and at work in the world around us. It's the conduit for messaging and receiving messages from God, a way to connect with him and receive all manner of information from the Creator of the universe. And if you've never experienced prayer this way, it's not hard to learn. You have a God who wants nothing more than to teach you.

If I'm certain of anything it's this: God wants to teach us how to pray. He is a personal God, a God of love, who wants to connect and communicate with us. This kind of connection and communion, though, won't happen overnight. It takes daily commitment.

Far too often prayer exists primarily in the realm of dutiful religious obligation—dry, powerless, and inert, expressed in boredom or fear more than anticipation. Do you pray only when the chips are down? When there's a mild life crisis? Is prayer relegated to the family meal, or to that nervous space just before the big test at school, or as you walk into the conference room for your annual review at work? These are all good times to communicate with the Creator of the universe, of course, but God doesn't want to hear from us just before dinner or a test, or during the scarier times of our lives; he also wants to hear from us throughout the day. He wants to connect with us in all the moments of life, big and small. How do I know? Because Jesus modeled this truth.

As you're reading through the Gospels, notice how Jesus' life—a life perfectly connected to the Father—was marked by prayer. (In your journal, keep a list of all the prayers Jesus prays. It is fascinating.) Prayer was part of his daily routine. He prayed for seemingly ordinary things: for children brought to him by the townspeople (Matt. 19:13), for meals (Matt. 14:19), for friends (John 17:1–25). He prayed before major events, too, like choosing the twelve disciples (Luke 6:12) and raising Lazarus from the dead (John 11:41). Jesus seemed to imagine prayer as essential to his life assignment. He understood prayer as a powerful tool for sustaining momentum in his life. And because he is both our Lord and our mentor, his pattern directs us toward a richer, fuller, more constant life of prayer.

Jesus didn't just model prayer; he invited his friends and followers into a life of prayer with him. He wanted them to experience the rewards of a God-oriented, God-connected life. He wanted them to communicate with the God who provides everything we need. So in his first public sermon, recorded early in the gospel of Matthew, Jesus taught the people how to pray. The method of prayer he taught wasn't complicated. In fact, he put it quite simply:

> "Ask and it will be given to you; seek and you will find; knock and the door will be opened to you. For everyone who asks receives; the one who seeks finds; and to the one who knocks, the door will be opened."
> (Matt. 7:7–8)

Jesus knew that an active prayer life leads to a vital connection with God, and that every good blessing, every need, every open door comes from God. Without prayer, then, how could we receive the rewards and blessings of God?

The early church took Christ's teachings on prayer seriously. It was their lifeline, and it served as a hallmark of the community. In the book of Acts, Luke writes that the first believers "devoted themselves to the apostles' teaching and to fellowship, to the breaking of bread and to prayer" (Acts 2:42). They prayed over new leaders of the church (Acts 6:6). Peter prayed before he raised Tabitha from the dead (Acts 9:40), and when he was imprisoned for preaching the gospel, the church "was earnestly praying to God for him" (Acts 12:5). In his letters to the early church, Paul, too, wrote specifically on prayer. To the church in Colossae, he wrote, "Devote yourselves to prayer, being watchful and thankful" (Col. 4:2). To the church at Philippi, he instructed them not to "be anxious about anything, but in every situation, by prayer and petition, with thanksgiving, present your requests to God" (Phil. 4:6). Prayer wasn't an afterthought in the early church—it was a central commitment, and part of what it meant to be Christian.

The Simple Way of Prayer

Prayer is important. If you've been in church for more than ten minutes, you've heard this truth. Still, each time I share about the power of prayer, people come to me confessing the deficiencies in their own prayer lives. They tell me they don't have enough time to pray every day, or that they don't like to pray in public because they're introverted. They claim prayer with their small group or spouse is difficult because they aren't eloquent enough or they don't know all the right spiritual lingo. I get it. But prayer is too important to leave in the shadow of our excuses. So let's learn. Let's grow in our expressions of prayer.

We learn to speak to God, just like we learned to speak to one another. As children, we communicated with phrases only a loving parent could understand. We asked our parents for our personal needs—food, comfort, or a fresh diaper—all in the hope that they would care for us. It wasn't until years into our lives that we began to communicate more fluidly, exchanging thoughts and ideas through conversation. Learning to pray begins in much the same way as learning to talk, with simple words or phrases that express recognized needs. The pattern is not wrong; it is a necessary part of development:

> *God, I need help . . .*
> *Lord, I am afraid, I do not know what to do . . .*
> *Lord, my family . . .*
> *God, my heart is broken . . .*

These are not incomplete prayers; they are genuine expressions of invitation, and the beginning of communication. So just as we learn to speak, we learn to listen. We learn to hear God's response, as we learned to hear our parents' response as children.

What is true physically is true spiritually. As you push

deeper into prayer, you'll begin to see God's answers, his work in your everyday life, and you'll gain his perspective. After all, Jesus said, "my sheep hear my voice . . . and they follow me" (John 10:27 KJV). As you grow in prayer, you'll learn to follow his responses.

The Power of a Few Sentences

Prayer can be intimidating, especially in public. But it doesn't have to be. Prayer can be both simple and powerful. Don't believe me? Consider Jesus' prayers.

In the gospel of Matthew, when the disciples came to Jesus and asked him how they should pray, he told them to keep it simple, not to "keep on babbling like pagans, for they think they will be heard because of their many words" (6:7). Instead, he showed how the best prayers were short and powerful. How short? Only four sentences. He said:

> *"Our Father in heaven,*
> *hallowed be your name,*
> *your kingdom come,*
> *your will be done,*
>   *on earth as it is in heaven.*
> *Give us today our daily bread.*
> *And forgive us our debts,*
>   *as we also have forgiven our debtors.*

And lead us not into temptation,
but deliver us from the evil one."

(Matt. 6:9–13)

It's a prayer that invokes God's holiness ("hallowed be your name"), his authority ("your kingdom come"), his provision ("give us . . . our daily bread"), his mercy ("forgive us our debts"), and his salvation ("deliver us from the evil one"). All that truth, all those requests are jammed into four sentences. That's not so complicated, is it?

But if four sentences are still too much, I have some good news for you. Jesus—our prayer model—often prayed even shorter prayers. In fact, he did a lot with one-sentence prayers. On the cross, he offered forgiveness to his accusers (and to you and me) with a sentence: "Father, forgive them, for they do not know what they are doing" (Luke 23:34). His last words were: "Father, into your hands I commit my spirit" (v. 46). And those were the words that lit the fuse on the resurrection, and ultimately, our salvation.

If Jesus' prayer life demonstrates anything, it's that a prayer doesn't have to be wordy or complicated. Our prayers can be short, sweet, and to the point. When Jesus raised Lazarus from the dead, he offered a three-word prayer: "Lazarus, come out!" (John 11:43). If I had been in charge of crafting the resurrection prayer, however, I probably would have created more fanfare. I would have turned it into an event, had a full band to lead a few worship choruses, then read some powerful passage of scripture (maybe about the resurrection of the dry bones in Ezekiel). I would have made space for a couple of healing testimonies, and then staged the big moment with a very wordy, super-holy prayer. All that pomp and circumstance—it's what humans do when we want to celebrate something. But Jesus was not about attracting attention. He showed us that prayer is focusing our attention on the God of all creation and his ability to do more than we ask or think. So do not despise short prayers; they can have tremendous impact.

Short, simple prayers—they don't seem so daunting, do they? But how do you incorporate short, simple, powerful prayers into your daily life? You can pray the Lord's Prayer as you go about the day, using it as a prompt to ask for your daily needs, for forgiveness, or for protection from temptation. You can use one-sentence prayers as you go about your day too. In fact, consider using these sample prayers throughout your day:

- Before you get out of bed in the morning, pray: *Lord, help me to honor you today.*
- When you pull into the parking lot at your work, pray: *Lord, allow me to be a light for you today.*
- When you walk in the front door of your home, pray: *God, thank you for my family.*
- When you put your head on your pillow at night, pray: *Lord, help me to rest in your watchful care.*

(In addition to these prayers, in the back of this book, I've provided a list of short prayers you can use as you go about your day.)

Prayers like these have transformed our church community as our faith has moved beyond the sanctuary and into our everyday lives. We've learned to pray these prayers over our families and coworkers in real time. If we see each other in the grocery store (the park, the ball field, or elsewhere), and one of us shares a need, the other will pray a simple prayer right there in the produce section. What's the result? When any sort of need arises—big, little, benign, or malignant—we're comfortable bringing it to God. We're comfortable asking him to intervene on our behalf. And we have seen that God responds in the most remarkable ways. Sometimes we get the answer we'd imagined, and other times we receive answers we didn't expect. But no matter the answer, we've come to see that we're not alone. The Creator of all things is walking with us through every chapter of our lives.

The God Who Answers

I was at the gym early one morning trying to complete my workout with a good attitude. I was on a chest-press machine, sweating and dreaming of Cracker Barrel, when a woman approached and asked for prayer. I thought I had looked too busy to pray, with sweat dripping and gasping for air. Couldn't she hear my muscles screaming for me to stop? Nevertheless, I let the weight down, stood, and asked what her request was. Her son was facing serious challenges and needed a breakthrough, she said. She didn't know what to do.

"Let's pray," I said. She immediately knelt in the middle of the gym, right in front of everyone. In this most competitive environment, I thought, *I'm not going to be outprayed by a stranger.* So I followed her lead. On our knees, in the middle of a group of strangers pumping iron, we prayed. Some days later, she found me again and reported her progress. Signs of breakthrough were on the horizon. Things were looking up.

In the following months, we prayed several times, often right there in the gym. In the process, I made a new friend, and I no longer see the gym as a place where prayer is awkward. The faith of a woman opened the door, and I just followed along. Prayer can be more than a conduit for making our requests known to God; it can be a conduit for community change.

When we don't pray, we forfeit the possibility of God's work in our lives and the lives of those around us. We miss opportunities to express our faith in ways that change the community. We fail to connect with him and receive his rewards. Though those rewards aren't always immediate or what we'd like, they're always good (James 1:17). So don't wait till all else has failed before resorting to prayer. Don't wait till a crisis comes. Commit now to pray every day, and you'll experience God in a new way. You'll sense his work in your family, your job, and the world around you. Your perspective will change as you see God answering prayers, opening doors, and giving good gifts. As you gain confidence in prayer, your faith will begin to grow. And when the dark days come, you'll have a new response with confidence in a God who delivers.

While developing your own vocabulary and confidence in prayer, borrow the prayers from this book. Use them as starter prayers. Create a new, normal pattern for learning to pray. Find your voice and your own unique ways of recognizing God in your life. Are you ready? Let's pray!

AN EXERCISE OF INTENT

1. Is your life marked by prayer? When was the last time you prayed without being prompted by a crisis? When was the last time you prayed for someone else, particularly when they weren't in a crisis?

2. Do you have difficulty praying with others? If so, write down the reasons and ask God to help you work through them.

3. Make a list of five people you know need prayer. Next to their names, jot a one-sentence prayer to

pray over them. Pray this prayer over them each morning or night. And the next time you see them, let them know you're praying for them.

A PRAYER FOR LEARNING TO PRAY

Heavenly Father, teach me to pray and to recognize your responses. Thank you for caring enough to be involved with my life. Open my heart to your presence in ways I have never known. Give me the courage to acknowledge you in every part of my life. May my life be pleasing in your sight. Amen.

PART THREE

INTENTIONAL FAITH: THE OUTWARD EXPRESSIONS OF FAITH

Each tree is recognized by its own fruit. People do not pick figs from thornbushes, or grapes from briers. A good man brings good things out of the good stored up in his heart, and an evil man brings evil things out of the evil stored up in his heart. For the mouth speaks what the heart is full of.

—Luke 6:44–45

Jesus reminds us that our personal faith is on display each day. The conditions of our hearts are visible through the actions and attitudes we express. Our private devotion is not really private at all; it is evident to anyone who is observing our lives.

Our homes, our business activities, even our recreational lives are all demonstrations of our belief system. The imagination that God will improve our lives, not diminish them, will enable us to invite him into each arena of our lives. We need the evidence of God in the midst of our lives, the most challenging parts, not just when we sit in a church service or have our devotional moments.

The following chapters will provide an opportunity to imagine God's involvement in some new ways. It may seem like he is intruding, stepping into arenas where your will has been supreme. Never forget, Jesus will improve your life and enhance your future. You never have to fear Jesus' involvement with your plans and activity.

SEVEN

INTEND TO HONOR GOD IN YOUR HOME

Lessons I learned at home have shaped my life. Many of those principles were not taught with words; they were lived out in the context of daily routines. Looking back, I was the beneficiary of choices my parents made for themselves. I suspect none of us understood the full implications of what was unfolding in the moment.

After a long day with farmers, horse breeders, and pet owners, Dad would walk through the front door, hug my mother, and help gather my brothers and me for dinner. Sitting down for dinner together was a family tradition that was unassailable. My mom invested in the effort to have dinner ready. My dad invested in the effort to ensure three boys were present and accounted for. I didn't realize it at the time, but dinner was the clearinghouse of the day's thoughts and activities. It was a learning forum, a calendar review, an intentional parental intervention, and a nourishing meal. House rules established that presence at the evening dinner table was mandatory for those who lived in the house, no matter our age.

It was the after-dinner habit that left a lasting impression on me. When dinner was complete and the kitchen cleaned, my parents would typically sit down and read their Bibles, often with a dialogue about whatever they were reading. No one was watching, and there was no enforcement involved. They simply chose to read their Bibles. I noticed. I didn't participate but wondered about the unusual behavior. I realized it was something that mattered to them, not because of public perception but because it was something they attached value to. Without issuing a family edict, they communicated a life-changing value to me: the pursuit of God was worthwhile!

I was aware enough of my friends' families to understand that my parents' choices were focused in less traditional paths. Most of their time was spent managing a small business, wrestling horses, maintaining a home, or corralling three boys. But when they had discretionary time—and there was not a great deal of it—they frequently directed their effort toward God. I expected more fishing, ball games, or boating.

Sometimes circumstances would dictate that we'd miss church. As a substitute, we would have family time. Someone would read a Bible story, then we'd ask questions. It was always pretty relaxed. More energy was spent on wrangling boys than on the exegesis. I remember a time we read the portion where Jesus turned water into wine. One of us asked if God still did that, and if so, could we pray for it. To my great surprise, my dad grabbed a coffee mug, filled it with water, and said, "Pray away!" To our disappointment there was no emerging merlot, although I'm pretty sure we would not have been encouraged to imbibe even if our prayer had been answered. It was my dad's permission to pray that surprised me. I was expecting a discussion on alcohol. My dad gave me permission to treat the Bible as a how-to guide— another significant nudge in the development of my faith. My parents attempted to practice what the Bible said, but even more, they taught us to believe it, to treat the things contained in its pages as if they were still possible.

Honoring God in the home, devoting time and attention to him, didn't feel like a unique approach back then. Our home had a faith component because we'd experienced God's grace. We understood how much we'd benefitted from his goodness, how he spared my mom's life and paved the way for our family to come to faith. As a result, there was no confusion about whom my parents served in the home. It'd be God first and everything else second. Although I was tempted to leave the faith behind from time to time in my early college years, as an adult, I found myself drawn back to God. Those early lessons were more profound than I had realized.

What You Do in Private Matters

We live in a society that's increasingly exposed. It seems nothing is private, and our entire lives are monitored and tracked. And so, we crave private spaces. "What you do in the privacy of your own home," society says, "is your business. After all, it doesn't impact anyone but you." This is an understandable response to our highly surveilled lives. Truth be told, though, who we are in private and what we do in our home are the primary contributors to who we can become beyond our home.

Our traditional approach to faith relegates God to a sixty-minute time slot on Sunday mornings, and reserves the rest of the time for ourselves. And the awkward truth of the modern age is that we have been reluctant to open our lives more fully to God, while we have willingly opened our lives to 24/7 connectivity for entertainment and diversion.

Who we are in private matters, and it will always come to light. In fact, Jesus taught, "There is nothing concealed that will not be disclosed, or hidden that will not be made known" (Luke 12:2). So the goal of our spiritual lives should be to let our public expressions of faith emerge out of the incubator of our private lives, because when they do, we're living the kind of life Christ rewards. How do I know? Because Jesus taught as much in the gospel of Matthew, saying that if we do what's right behind closed doors, "your Father, who sees what is done in secret, will reward you" (6:4). It is a wonderful promise. Private discipline will be rewarded in the open. Each time we choose a God-response behind closed doors, we are making an investment in a better future.

The great men and women of faith in the Bible knew as much. Take Joshua, for example. Knowing Moses was nearing the end of his ministry, Joshua, Moses' successor, gathered the people of Israel and recounted the history of God's deliverance when the people served him whole-heartedly. He then issued this charge: "If serving the LORD seems undesirable to you, then choose for yourselves this day whom you will serve. . . . But as for me and my household, we will serve the LORD" (Josh. 24:15). The people responded, saying they wanted to honor God in their households too. So Joshua doubled down: "Then . . . throw away the foreign gods that are among you and yield your hearts to the LORD, the God of Israel" (v. 23).

Joshua was clear: If we want the blessings of God, we have to honor him in our homes. And if we want to honor God in our homes, we cannot hide our foreign gods in our closets. We cannot love the things the world loves. Honoring God in our homes requires turning from the things of the world—like consumerism, pornography, ungodly attitudes, and secular ideologies—and turning toward God.

The Reward of Honoring God in the Home

How could you live a life of private devotion? Here's the hard truth: the hardest place in the world to take your faith is home. The people you live with day in and day out have seen you holler and cuss and kick the dog across the room. They probably have seen you watch things you ought not watch, might know just how addicted you are to your iPhone, and certainly know your propensity to overwork. The people in your home know things about you you'd never want leaked. So when you tell them of your commitment to seek the Lord, to make honoring him a priority in your home, they may break out in laughter. They may even look at you with derision. That's okay. We all have to start somewhere. But as you begin to honor God in the home, my guess is that they'll like the changes they see. They might even decide to join you.

My parents made a decision to honor God in our home, even when no one was looking. It wasn't perfect, of course. There were times they lost their tempers and grew impatient. I'm sure there were times they didn't read or watch the most spiritual things. Still, my parents led by example, honoring God in the private moments of their lives, and as a result, I took their faith seriously.

"Sure, but you're a pastor," you might say, "and you have supernatural willpower as a man of the cloth." Not so. I'm just as flawed as the rest of you, and just as capable of missing the mark. The flip side of that coin, though, is that you're just as capable of honoring God in your home, even if you are alone. Take Melody, for example, a single woman in our church who made a commitment to honor God in her home. Being unmarried and living alone, she shared how easy it'd be to live a life of public faith, all while hiding her private life from others. "I'm the gatekeeper," she said to me during a meeting. "I could easily slink behind that gate and hide. I could watch whatever I want, say whatever I want, and do whatever I want." But she made a decision that, as the gate-keeper, as the one responsible for what comes in and out of her home, she would do her best to guard her mind and heart by keeping out anything that might dishonor God. And this private devotion expresses itself in public, in the way she serves, in her attitudes, and in the way she loves others.

So whether you're married with children, single and living alone, or the stepparent in a blended household, no matter what your situation looks like, it's up to you to lead the way in honoring God in the home. If you haven't been doing your part, I'm inviting you to take an incremental step in the right direction. What might that step look like?

- Repent of the times you haven't honored God in your home, the times you've ignored God, the times you've lost your temper or lashed out, or the times you've allowed things into your house you shouldn't have.
- Choose to protect your home from anything that dishonors God.

- Offer a simple prayer each day as you come home from work: *God, may you be glorified in my home tonight, and may I live with integrity.*

Make the commitment to honor God in your home and see what happens. You cannot cause everyone in your home to choose God's best. You can only determine to honor God within your own heart and entrust others to God's watchful care. Honoring God is not about growing beyond temptation and human frailty; it's about learning to invite God into your weakest moments and trusting him to enable you to overcome. God's faithfulness to respond to your invitation changes your future. When you develop a foundation of honoring God in the quiet places of your life, it provides the momentum for honoring God in the more public parts of your journey. The transforming power of the Holy Spirit begins from the inside out. Your faith is determined by an inward choice, not by outward obedience to rules. So, too, your intent to honor God in your home is a first step to experiencing his power in a broader way.

AN EXERCISE OF INTENT

1. Behind closed doors, when no one is looking, are you honoring the Lord? If not, what are the things that distract you, that keep you from living a life

aligned with God's heart? In your journal, make an honest list of the distractions, then commit to eliminating them.

2. What would your husband, wife, or children say about the life you live in secret? Would they say you do your best to honor the Lord, or that your private life is not aligned with the expression of your faith? Make a sincere assessment, and if you haven't been honoring God in the home, talk with your spouse and family members about the changes you could make.

3. In your journal, list three ways you can be intentional about teaching your children to honor God in your home. And do those things for the next one hundred days.

A PRAYER FOR MY HOME

Heavenly Father, you are the initiator of home and family. I pray that your presence would fill my home. Give me the wisdom to make choices behind closed doors that bring your great blessings into my life. I know nothing is hidden from your sight. Direct my steps so that they are pleasing to you. May the peace of God and the joy of the Lord fill my home each day. In Jesus' name, amen.

EIGHT

INTEND TO WORK
WITH INTEGRITY

I intend to work with integrity. Not because I have to or because someone expects me to, but because work is an expression of my relationship with God. When we are first introduced to God in the opening chapter of Genesis, he is busy bringing order out of chaos. At the end of six days, God rests from his work of creation.

> By the seventh day God had finished the work he had been doing; so on the seventh day he rested from all his work. (Gen. 2:2)

My attitude toward work reflects my attitude toward God as much as my attitude toward more formal expressions of worship.

Dad was a farm boy at heart, which made him the perfect veterinarian. He loved the job and loved helping animals. He took calls morning, noon, and night. When he wasn't tending to our neighbors' animals, though, he was tending to outside chores around our house—feeding our livestock, managing our fields, maintaining our equipment. There was enough work to go around, and Dad, knowing the value of that work, wanted to teach it to us.

Our relocation to Tennessee had been, at least in part, to provide my brothers and me with an opportunity to learn lessons about work that were not as readily available in a more urban environment. So my earliest memories are colored with following my dad to work. Sometimes I would be entrusted with carrying some of the tools or medicines needed while he visited the barns to tend to the show horses. I'd watch in wonder as Dad tended to a horse's lameness, colic, or any other problem these equine athletes needed help with.

On other occasions I would join my dad in the barn at home. There were always stalls to clean, horses to feed, or other tasks to do to help the animals flourish. I was raised to see work not as an onerous burden to be dreaded but as an adventure in learning and experience. I now know my father gave my brothers and me a tremendous gift on those days we were climbing fences and catching horses for evaluation and treatment. He taught us the dignity of work.

At this point a bit of confession is needed. I often

chafed at the assignments I received. I was tasked with hauling hay out of the field and stacking it in the barn or cleaning stalls (not the most glamorous of summer jobs), while my friends were lifeguards, working at a golf course, or maybe just spending time at a nearby lake. My attitude was not always stellar. Far more than I knew, I was in training.

If my upbringing taught me anything, it was the value of work. As I grew into adulthood, I began to see that hard work has more than just physical and psychological rewards, like a salary and a sense of accomplishment. As I learned the Scriptures, I began to notice all the spiritual blessings of work—and the curses of laziness. I read Paul's writings to Timothy, where he wrote that the one who does not provide for his family has "denied the faith and is worse than an unbeliever" (1 Tim. 5:8). I noticed how the psalmists and the writers of the Proverbs promised abundance to those who worked hard, and how work was described as a sort of worship to the Lord. As I read the Scriptures, I became convinced that there is a spiritual aspect to work, one I hadn't considered as a kid.

The Changing View of Work

According to a survey by Deloitte, today's youngest generation of employees is more disaffected with modern business and trusts companies less. The survey reports a "negative shift in millennials' feelings about business' motivations and ethics."[1] Moreover, the survey states:

> Forty-three percent of millennials envision leaving their jobs within two years; only 28 percent seek to stay beyond five years. The 15-point gap is up from seven points last year. Employed Gen Z respondents express even less loyalty, with 61 percent saying they would leave within two years if given the choice.[2]

I don't see these stats as negative, though some might. I think they reflect a tremendous opportunity. The emerging generation needs a purpose beyond a paycheck. They prefer work that satisfies rather than work that simply pays well. They want to experience life, express creativity, and experience personal growth. All of which, if properly directed, can be expressions of a meaningful faith, particularly when expressed in the workplace.

There are challenges to expressing your faith in the workplace, though, even if you find a meaningful, purpose-filled career. A recent study cited by *Inc.* magazine found that approximately 70 percent of American workers admit to being distracted on the job, with 16 percent admitting near-constant distraction. In the survey, 43 percent of baby boomers, 57 percent of Gen X-ers, and 78 percent of millennials and Gen Z-ers admitted to technological distraction in the workplace.[3] More startling is that 36 percent of millennials admit to spending two hours or more on their smartphones tending to personal matters (almost ten hours per week).

What was once held in the highest esteem—the value of an honest day's wage for an honest day's work—has been hijacked by the intrusions of the digital age. But a scriptural view of work might solve our problems. It fills our careers with meaning and provides an invitation to connect with, identify with, and worship God. With this view, how could we give our time to meaningless distractions?

God's View of Work

In the book of Genesis, we're introduced to a God who is hard at work. For five days he worked to create the heavens, the earth, the plants, the celestial bodies, and all the animals. On the sixth day, he worked to create the pinnacle of creation, man and woman. He made humankind in his own image, then gave them their first work assignment: cultivate, care for, and steward God's creation *with* him (Gen. 1:27–28). This call to work has continued ever since, and we see it play out throughout the Scriptures. Moses was given work to do, namely, to lead the people of Israel out of captivity in Egypt. God called Deborah to deliver the counsel of God to the people of Israel. Jesus called the unscrupulous, over-collecting, unfair tax man, Zacchaeus, to leave his dirty business and work with integrity and generosity. As a bi-vocational minister, Paul made tents to provide for himself and the early church as he preached the gospel.

Every follower of God has an assignment, even if it's not as grand as that of Moses or Deborah or Zacchaeus or Paul. We've been put in this specific time and specific place for a specific work assignment. It might be tending to a career as a teacher or a veterinarian or a used car salesman. It might be to stay at home with your kids or to care for your aging parents. It might have huge, far-reaching implications or it may be unsung. No matter, though, your assignment is to be an expression of the heart of God. In fact, the way you work—teach, give veterinary care, sell cars, parent, or tend to your parents—is a much more accurate reflection of your heart for God than how you present yourself at church.

How do I know? In the book of Colossians, Paul shared that all our work is to be oriented toward God as a form of worship. He wrote,

Whatever you do, work at it with all your heart, as working for the Lord, not for human masters, since you know that you will receive an inheritance from the Lord as a reward. It is the Lord Christ you are serving. (Col. 3:23–24)

Those verses convey an incredible truth if we can receive it. You may have human bosses (and if you're a stay-at-home mother, you have one who cannot speak in complete sentences). But ultimately, you don't work for the party checking your time sheets or signing your checks. Your employer is a loving, eternal, benevolent Father who wants you to carry his love into the world through your assignment. How you work, then, shows how much you think of the assignment he's given you, and consequently, how much you think of him.

Working as if it's a form of worship can change the way you think about your occupation. It can change the way you view your bosses, your coworkers, your customers. By seeing them as potential recipients of God's love, as witnesses to your worship, you'll begin to understand how you've been placed in their lives for a particular season and reason. If you live into that understanding, you'll notice changes in your daily interactions. You'll begin to see people at work as people to love, instead of as obstacles to negotiate through.

Work is not a new four-letter word. It's an opportunity to worship and to share the good news of God with the world around us. So let's not complain about our bosses, our coworkers, or the people we serve. Let's not be distractible, half-productive workers either. Let's be responsive to the assignments given to us, working as hard as we can to make the most of the opportunities we have before us. If we do, we'll reap the rewards of God-oriented work.

How to Work with God Instead of for Yourself

Our jobs won't always fulfill us. Our assignments won't always fill us with a sense of accomplishment or appreciation or purpose. Some days my job just feels like a thankless routine, with an endless line of people holding high expectations. But even when you're discontent in your career, ask yourself some pointed questions:

- Do I recognize my current occupation as an assignment from the Lord, or do I work with a chip on my shoulder?
- Do I have a joyful disposition in the workplace or a bad attitude?
- Am I creating or contributing to a culture of godliness or one of careless indifference?

If, after careful examination, you find you're not working as unto the Lord, offer this prayer of repentance:

Lord, I know my job is an assignment from you. I confess I haven't worked that assignment as an act of worship to you, and as a result, I've missed out on the spiritual and tangible rewards you offer. Change my heart and my attitude. Teach me to work as if you're my boss.

After you've repented, begin each workday with a one-sentence prayer: *God, help me to work as if I'm working for you today.* Then see what happens. See if you experience more job fulfillment, or if you reap more tangible rewards. See if your bosses or employees take notice. When they ask what accounts for your changed attitude and effort, be honest, and tell them your faith led you. Then watch their reactions and see if it leads to more opportunities to share the Scripture with them.

As you move into your one-hundred-day journey of faith, make it your aspiration to join God in his work. Be a leader at your workplace, in the marketplace, and show how your work can be an expression of your devotion to God. Together, let's demonstrate how working as an act of worship leads to the kind of life God rewards. Then, let's reap the benefits, both spiritual and tangible.

AN EXERCISE OF INTENT

1. Are you distracted at work? Do you find yourself sidetracked by nonwork-related activities? In your journal, make an honest list of those things that tend to distract you.

2. After reviewing the list, ask how you might be able to overcome those distractions. Do you need to leave your phone in your desk drawer? Put filters on your screens? Limit your trips to the watercooler for sports talk? Make a specific list

and commit to following through with it for the one-hundred-day journey of faith.

3. If Jesus had your job, how would he work? What things are you doing that he would do? What things would he refrain from doing? Be as specific as possible, then set your sights on working as he would over the next one hundred days.

A PRAYER FOR DELIVERANCE FROM HOPELESS EFFORT

Heavenly Father, awaken me to your purposes for my life. In the midst of my routine and responsibilities, help me to see your possibilities and assignments. Forgive me when I grumble and complain. I trust you for your provision in my life—resources, strength, patience, whatever is needed—to enable me to thrive. I know you will be faithful to me. In Jesus' name, amen.

NINE

INTEND TO TEACH THE YOUNGER GENERATION

I was surprised in a men's Bible study when Steve, a burly, square-jawed, and somewhat stoic vascular surgeon spoke up. He wasn't new to the faith, but for the first time in his adult life, he (and his wife) had decided to pursue God with intention. He committed to do whatever the Lord asked of him, whether large or small. Among the things God asked him to do, he said, was to teach his children to love and honor God in their everyday lives. As he spoke, he pulled a small canister from his pocket and held it up, smiling my way. It was a canister I recognized. In fact, I'd given it to him.

The previous Father's Day, I'd given every dad in our congregation a similar pocket canister of anointing oil. It was an out-of-the-ordinary gift, something most dads in our congregation wouldn't know what to do with. So I explained how they could use it: "Every day, whether in the morning before you walk out the door, or at night before you tuck your kids into bed, anoint your kids with the oil and pray a simple prayer over them." I reminded the men in our congregation that they didn't have to pray some long and drawn-out prayer. It could be a sentence, something like, *I bless your day in Jesus' name* or *Lord, let us rest tonight*. I assured them it might feel odd at first, but it's a way of demonstrating, teaching, and passing on the faith to the next generation, a way of demonstrating how to honor God in the little moments of life.

In the Bible study, Steve shared how he hadn't used the anointing oil at first. But as he and his wife considered the ways they could teach their kids to honor God, he had an idea. When the school year started, he'd take the kids to school each morning, and before dropping them off, he'd turn, anoint them with oil, and offer a one-sentence blessing over each of them every day. He committed himself to this routine for the rest of the year, and though it'd been awkward at first, the kids seemed to enjoy it. Was it making a difference in their days? He wasn't sure, but regardless, he was committed to the practice. At least mostly.

After a few weeks of his new routine, on a particularly rushed day, the morning anointing and blessing slipped his mind. Once at school, he hustled the kids out of the car, set his gear into drive, and was ready to pull away when he heard a knock on the passenger-side window. It was his grade school–aged son. As the window rolled down, his son asked, "Dad, you forgot to anoint me this morning. Do you have time?"

As Steve shared the story, the atmosphere in the room shifted. The men softened. One said he, too, wanted to leave the same sort of legacy to his children. Then another said the same. We pushed into conversation and processed how such a simple action could have such a profound impact. Blessing the younger generation on a regular basis, in the midst of our busy lives, was a simple way to pass the faith from one generation to the next. It became apparent that passing our faith down didn't have to be a complicated thing. And it wasn't relegated only to parents with young children. In fact, this opportunity exists for all of us, whether we're spending time with our own children, our stepchildren, or those we mentor. As the discussion progressed, we realized we freely share what we feel is important. So why not share our faith? If we didn't step forward with our faith, how would Christianity survive the onslaught of cultural pressure? How would it outlive us?

It wouldn't.

Teaching the Younger Generation, Preserving the Faith

I've heard it said that it only takes three generations for an idea or practice to be lost. We naively assume our values and lifestyles will persist unchallenged, passed down from generation to generation. But consider this simple example: my grandfather provided for his family by working in the fields with a team of horses, but these days, most of us would have no idea how to use a team of horses to work the fields. If we had to harness a team or hitch up a wagon, we wouldn't be able to do it. Why? Because those skills have slipped away.

A recent experience with a millennial staff member reminded me of the pace of change, and of how quickly knowledge can be lost. James is a young staffer in our accounting department. He's brighter and more aware than most his age. He is the type of character I might call street-wise. In a normal office conversation, I made some reference to the Yellow Pages. He stared back at me, blinking. Noting his confusion, I asked whether he had ever used a phone book. He said, "Only as a booster seat when I visited my grandparents as a child." I pressed further and asked if he had ever used a pay phone. He admitted he had not. In fact, he said he'd never seen a telephone booth except in the movies, and if push came to shove, he wouldn't know how to use one.

"What about a paper map? Have you ever used one of those?" I asked.

Shaking his head, he laughed.

It's a simple example of an ancient truth: without education, without some intentional act to preserve knowledge, the things we take for granted today will be forgotten tomorrow.

Our traditions? Yes. Our everyday knowledge? You bet. Our faith? The same. If we don't pass on what we've learned, if we don't make a concerted effort to teach the next generation how to honor God, the truths we once took for granted will be distant memories.

When you've lived into the life God rewards, when you've experienced the fruit of those rewards in your own life, it's natural to want to pass that faith down to the next generation. You'll want your children, stepchildren, grandchildren, or those younger people in your community to experience the same kind of life outcomes you've experienced. Desires aside, though, teaching the younger generation to honor God and his commands is a biblical mandate.

Consider the story of Moses. After leading the great exodus of Israel from Egypt, after receiving the Ten Commandments from God on the mountain, he led the people on a journey to the land promised to them by God. And standing on the edge of that land, just before he passed the mantle of leadership to his protégé, Joshua, he reminded the people—the younger generation—of the law given by God:

> These are the commands, decrees and laws the LORD your God directed me to teach you to observe in the land that you are crossing the Jordan to possess, so that you, your children and their children after them may fear the LORD your God as long as you live by keeping

all his decrees and commands that I give you, and so that you may enjoy long life. (Deut. 6:1–2)

And though the implication was clear—the people were to teach their children the law of the Lord—he made it explicit: "These commandments that I give you today are to be on your hearts. Impress them on your children. Talk about them when you sit at home and when you walk along the road, when you lie down and when you get up" (vv. 6–7).

If they kept the faith, if they passed it down from generation to generation, there'd be great reward. Moses promised:

Then the LORD your God will keep his covenant of love with you, as he swore to your ancestors. He will love you and bless you and increase your numbers. He will bless the fruit of your womb, the crops of your land—your grain, new wine and olive oil—the calves of your herds and the lambs of your flocks in the land he swore to your ancestors to give you. You will be blessed more than any other people; none of your men or women will be childless, nor will any of your livestock be without young. (7:12–14)

According to Moses, passing our faith to the younger generation held real and tangible rewards for the here and now. I think the same promises hold true today.

Jesus had a heart for the younger generation too. In the book of Matthew, the disciples asked him who was the greatest in the kingdom. Instead of giving the answer they expected, he called a child to his lap. Pointing to the child, he said the children were the most important people in the kingdom of God. And as if to drive the point home, he shared the consequences for failing to teach them how to follow God: "If anyone causes one of these little ones—those who believe in me—to stumble, it would be better for them to have a large millstone hung around their neck and to be drowned in the depths of the sea" (Matt. 18:6). While it's a harsh image, consider the implications. If we don't teach the younger generation how to honor God, aren't we leaving them to their own devices? Aren't we leaving them unprotected in the struggle with life's challenges? It's a sobering thought, one that moves me from theoretical into action.

For the record, it's worth noting that the child on Jesus' lap wasn't his own. So Jesus wasn't limiting the responsibility of teaching the younger generation to those living within the four walls of our home. Jesus himself was the beneficiary of a borrowed dad. Joseph was recruited to be part of a blended family that included Jesus. Sometimes we feel reluctant to lead with our faith because our family circumstances are not perfect. Yet even Jesus' family was blended.

I believe Jesus wanted his disciples to understand that they shared a responsibility to all the little ones, to all the younger generation. Thus, though passing the faith to the next generation is a primary assignment for the parents, it's not limited to parents. We all have a stake in the faith development of the next generation. After all, when we're long gone, they'll be the Christian leaders. We should equip them to impact the generations that follow them with a meaningful faith!

A Faith Bigger Than Rocky Top

In Tennessee, it's hard to find a child who doesn't know the song "Rocky Top," one of the official state songs and a fight song for the University of Tennessee Volunteers. Why? I might argue it's because we've trained them up in the way they should go, at least as far as athletic devotion goes. We've equipped the generation to carry the torch of fanaticism for the Volunteers, despite the fact that our beloved team hasn't had a truly significant season since Noah's ark found dry ground on Mount Ararat. And if we can train the little people in our lives to show such great devotion to a state athletic team, it stands to reason we could teach them even greater devotion to the God of the universe.

More than stewards of sports fanaticism, we're stewards of the Christian faith, and God has called us to pass that faith down the line. We can model to the children in our communities a love and honor for God and an admiration for the godly men and women of faith in their lives. They will recognize our enthusiasm (or lack thereof) for the kind of life God rewards. If we neglect this opportunity, our families, churches, and nation will suffer the consequences. But how do we pass the faith down the line? How do we teach the younger generation to honor God and his people? Certainly not by imposing mandatory hour-long Bible studies on those who lack the ability to escape our influences. Instead, we pass the faith down in small, simple, sometimes covert ways. Consider trying the following:

- Recognize the ways you've failed to teach the faith to your kids or grandkids, then confess them to God, and ask him to help you see new opportunities.
- Pray over your meals before eating.
- Before you walk in the house in the evening, thank God for your family and the sacred trust they represent. Your private prayers will help establish new attitudes.
- Before leaving the house in the morning, simply invite God in by praying, *God, bless my family today. They are your gift to me.*
- Routinely offer simple, one-sentence prayers over the young people in your life, such as, *God, thank you for Susie. Help her to have a great day at school.*

Remember, it doesn't have to be some grandiose gesture, and I'm not suggesting some drastic, overnight changes in your attitude toward teaching the younger generation. If you've never made any intentional efforts to pass the faith down, I'm not asking you to sign up to teach a weekly Sunday school class or register as a volunteer mentor in your community. I'm inviting you to take a small, incremental step into the privileged life of a person of faith. You can do it. When you do, you'll experience the joy that comes with adding God-momentum to another life. What's more, when we help the younger generation to love, serve, and honor God, we build stronger communities of faith and better family ties, and we welcome the blessings of God into generations to follow. Those kinds of faithful communities have been making a difference since Noah's sons helped with God's assignment to build an ark. Our generation is no less critical. I pray we will cultivate the expressed intent to invest in those who follow us!

As we continue to pursue the life God rewards, as we experience the benefits of it, let's teach those who come behind us to do the same. Let's determine to contribute to a lasting legacy of faith and watch what God does with our simple efforts.

AN EXERCISE OF INTENT

1. Who are the younger people in your life? Are they children you're raising in your home, the

students you teach, the young worker who's coming up behind you? Identify those younger people and name them specifically.

2. Consider the names you listed. Ask yourself how you're teaching them the things of faith. Write down three ways you can encourage each of them in faith over the next week.

3. Just as we need to be teaching the younger generation, we also need teachers. Is there anyone further along in their life of faith whom you can seek for wisdom and counsel? Approach them over the next few weeks and ask whether they would be willing to pour faith into you.

A PRAYER FOR THE CHILDREN AND YOUNG PEOPLE

Heavenly Father, you are a father to the fatherless and a comfort to the orphans. Forgive me for my shortcomings in caring for the generations following me. Redeem the days I have wasted, open doorways of opportunity, and grant me the boldness needed to honor you. May my life be an encouragement to others. Holy Spirit, direct me in pathways you can reward. In Jesus' name, amen.

PART FOUR

INTENTIONAL FAITH: GAINING SPIRITUAL HEALTH

Create in me a pure heart, O God,
and renew a steadfast spirit within me.

—Psalm 51:10

Spiritual health is very similar to physical health—it requires attention and effort. We cannot earn our way into heaven, but our responses to God can open or close doors of opportunity. As we begin to walk toward God, he initiates changes in our hearts. We benefit from a power greater than our own determination.

Throughout the Scriptures, God demonstrates the importance of the heart. The writer of Proverbs instructs, "Above all else, guard your heart, for everything you do flows from it" (4:23). The psalmist writes, "May these words of my mouth and this meditation of my heart be pleasing in your sight" (19:14). In the book of Matthew, Jesus teaches, "Blessed are the pure in heart, for they will see God" (5:8).

Aligning our hearts with the heart of God requires the development of certain attitudes: generosity, forgiveness, perseverance, and a willingness to cooperate with the Holy Spirit. These heart attitudes are often contrary to our natural human responses. Read through the following chapters and ask God to help align your heart with his. It's okay to tell him the truth. God can withstand the shock of your reality.

Remember, an accurate diagnosis is the first step toward improved health.

TEN

INTEND TO PRACTICE FORGIVENESS

From the earliest age, there were things I knew: adults would one day recognize pecan pie and chocolate as appropriate breakfast foods; I would be spending summer days exploring the creek and trekking through the woods; and I would become a doctor.

My dad had gone back to veterinary school when I was two years old and graduated when I was seven. I watched as he worked hard to achieve his dream of caring for animals. I listened as he recited medical facts about various creatures. I observed as he spent long hours poring over textbooks. And I saw him leave early and often return home late. I spent my youth enthusiastically serving as a vet's helper, although I suspect I was frequently more of a liability than an asset.

When it was time to formalize my career choice, I had

clarity. Though I loved the thought of practicing medicine, and I loved animals, I didn't love the idea of combining the two. I didn't want to perform surgery on livestock; I wanted to perform surgery on humans. So the minute I entered school, I was academically focused, particularly on math and science classes.

I enrolled in Oral Roberts University in Tulsa, Oklahoma, with the focus of a man who knew his future. I oriented my entire world—my calendar, study hours, and social circles—around doing what it took to have the letters *MD* after my name, which is no small task. If you've ever known a physician, you know that medical school is difficult and taxing, and that many who begin never finish. College professors, most of whom have doctorates, see themselves as the gatekeepers to medical school and, ultimately, to the medical profession. They take it upon themselves to weed out those who won't (or shouldn't) make the cut. Driving attrition was the name of their game, and they'd call out students, telling them they weren't good enough or capable enough or smart enough. Their criticisms were harsh, their tempers hot, and on more than one occasion, I found myself angry and frustrated at the deliberate stress they created. It wasn't just me, though. Many of my premed friends felt the same way, and when they complained, I gave them my stock speech: "Blow it off. That sorry so-and-so is not God, and you should tell him as much."

It was us against them. The students versus the professors.

It was the rivalry that drove me, that poured gasoline on the fire of my ambition. What I didn't realize, however, was that it was fueling a hidden bitterness, resentment, and anger, along with a host of other destructive responses.

By Christmas break of my junior year, my incoming class of premeds had dwindled down to a few dozen. I was surviving the academic rigors by running salary projections and planning which sports car I'd buy after completing my residency. Although I'd once been enamored with the idea of being a doctor, it was no longer solely about the profession but about beating the professors. It was personal.

I spent that Christmas break with my parents in Murfreesboro, and before the break ended, Aunt Mary came to visit. She had been a longtime family friend, a missionary who'd spent years in Cuba before the Communist regime took over. She was all but venerated in our home. She was also an admirer of Oral Roberts ministry. So when she heard I was driving back to Tulsa to begin a new semester, she asked if she could come along and visit the campus. There was not a polite way to decline, so I had a guest for the trip.

We set out to make what I thought would be a nine-hour trip from Murfreesboro to Tulsa. But somewhere in Arkansas, we ran headlong into winter weather; snow and sleet were coming down in sheets. To make matters worse, my heater went out, so I gave Aunt Mary a stack of coats to bundle up in. She snuggled under those coats, peeking out from time to time to ask a question about my studies. I told her about the rigorous program, the attrition rate, and the professors who considered themselves gods. She listened, offering little advice. Fourteen very cold and tired hours later, we pulled into Tulsa, half-frozen and heavy-eyed. I took her to a hotel near campus, ready to give her the boot and get up to my dorm room. But before she got out of the car, she asked, "Can we pray?"

I thought, *Pray? We'd had fourteen hours to pray and you didn't mention it once.* But being southern, I was taught to be polite, and not wanting to upset Aunt Mary, I said, "Sure, I'd love to."

After helping her get checked in, we sat down by the desk in her room, and I said, "Let's pray."

Before we could, though, she said, "I've listened to you all day, and you're an angry young man. In fact, I think you hate some of your professors. Do you think you could forgive them?"

Without thinking twice, I said, "I don't intend to. That anger motivates me. It gives me the drive to prove those people wrong and make it into medical school."

That's when Aunt Mary did what she was so good at doing. She nodded, then asked whether I'd considered what God might have to say about my anger. I didn't say anything, a tacit admission that I had not. She launched into the scriptures about forgiveness, and how it was a predicate to living the kind of life God rewards. She spent over two hours with me, telling me how God expected us to forgive those who accuse, intimidate, or hurt us. She shared how unforgiveness roots into our lives and poisons us. The bitterness and anger that I thought was the pathway to an objective goal actually held me in bondage, she said. It was a life lesson, and at the end, she asked if she could lead me in prayers of forgiveness. I agreed. We peeled back the layers of my anger, and I spoke forgiveness over many of my professors.

But after she whispered her amen, things took an unexpected turn. Aunt Mary asked, "Have you ever thought about the ministry?"

I assured her I hadn't. In fact, I told her ministry was the farthest thing from my mind.

"Are you sure?" she asked.

"I'm absolutely sure. You must be tired," I said.

With that, she smiled and thanked me for the ride, and I returned to my dorm.

The Power of Anger, the Power of Forgiveness

Anger, bitterness, and resentment are powerful things. So powerful, in fact, modern medicine has studied their effects on the body. In an article posted on the Johns Hopkins Medicine website, Dr. Karen Swartz, director of the Mood Disorders Adult Consultation Clinic at the Johns Hopkins Hospital, states, "There is an enormous physical burden to being hurt and disappointed."[1] The article goes on:

Chronic anger puts you into a fight-or-flight mode, which results in numerous changes in heart rate, blood pressure and immune response. Those changes, then, increase the risk of depression, heart disease and diabetes, among other conditions. Forgiveness, however, calms stress levels, leading to improved health.[2]

According to Dr. Swartz, the practice of forgiveness is "an active process in which you make a conscious decision to let go of negative feelings whether the person deserves it or not." It's a practice that leads to deeper empathy and compassion, and ultimately, has certain health benefits.[3]

It's not just medical professionals who understand the power of letting go. Plenty of everyday people do too. I heard a comedian on late-night TV say he had learned the secret to happiness: let go of anger. He said when you hold on to anger, it puts you and them in a cage. But while you are angry, the person you are angry at is dancing. Forgiveness will unlock the cage. I never expected spiritual counsel from late-night talk shows, but I found some. As this comedian spoke about releasing people from his anger, he gave the distinct impression that he hadn't just set others free, but he'd also set himself free. Free from what? From anger, bitterness, self-criticism, and self-doubt so many of us carry with us. His heart was light. He was comfortable with who he was and the criticisms he received from others.

If you've lived more than a day on this planet, you've

discovered this hard truth: people hurt people. Sometimes the pains inflicted are intentional: the abuse suffered at the hands of a parent, the harsh words by a competitive co-worker, the angry words hurled by a spouse in the heat of the moment. Sometimes they're accidental: the stray remark made in conversation, a loved one failing to meet unspoken expectations, the lack of attention from a busy pastor, parent, or friend. Evil people hurt people, but so do good people. I've been hurt by good people in my life, and I've hurt a fair share of folks along the way too. And because I've hurt people, even if unintentionally, I'm in as much need of forgiveness as anyone else, both from those I've hurt and from God.

When it comes to forgiveness, there are a few liberating truths expressed in the Bible. What are those truths?

The First Liberating Truth

Extending and receiving forgiveness require us to sacrifice our sense of entitlement to anger and bitterness, and to cultivate a tender heart. If you're anything like me, which is to say human, you've most certainly nursed anger toward another. You've likely made elaborate plans to ignore someone who's hurt you or formulated the most scathing rant for the next time you run into them in the supermarket. But often, which is to say always, these best-laid plans for demonstrating your anger and bitterness do nothing more than lock you in your own prison of hate and resentment.

Paul counseled an alternative path, though. He instructed the members of the church in Ephesus to "Get rid of all bitterness, rage and anger . . . along with every form of malice. Be kind and compassionate to one another, forgiving each other, just as in Christ God forgave you" (Eph. 4:31–32). By getting rid of bitterness, anger, and the like, by keeping a tender heart, you bring freedom into your own life.

What is less apparent is that by holding on to anger against others, we entrap ourselves. Sometimes we are angry at God because of our circumstances. Forgiveness toward others, toward God, and even toward ourselves brings liberty.

The Second Liberating Truth

Receiving forgiveness requires us to sacrifice our pride, and to approach others and God in loving humility. In the gospel of Luke, we are told Jesus was at a dinner party when a sinful woman approached him, knelt at his feet, wet his feet with her tears, dried them with her hair, and anointed him with perfume. The religious leaders at the table judged the woman silently, but Jesus knew their hearts. He said to them, "I tell you, her many sins have been forgiven—as her great love has shown. But whoever has been forgiven little loves little" (Luke 7:47). The religious leaders, the men who took pride in dotting every i of the law, found themselves at the end of Jesus' rebuke, while the woman who bowed in humility was praised. Why? Because she was willing to go so far as to publicly express her gratitude and appreciation for the mercy she had received; she was willing to approach Jesus in humility. We should be willing to do the same, both with Jesus and with others.

The Third Liberating Truth

God's forgiveness extends as far as we extend forgiveness to others. Consider Jesus' teaching on forgiveness in his Sermon on the Mount. Just after teaching his disciples to pray, he said, "Forgive us our debts, as we also have forgiven our debtors" (Matt. 6:12). "For if you forgive other people when they sin against you, your heavenly Father will also forgive you. But if you do not forgive others their sins, your Father will not forgive your sins" (vv. 14–15). If you want God to release you from your debts, your sins, you have to be willing to release the debts of others. It's nonnegotiable.

The Fourth Liberating Truth

There is one last liberating truth: we need to forgive God. Seasons of life arrive filled with unwanted things, such as sickness, disappointment, broken relationships, premature deaths. Facing life's challenges that seem unfair, uninvited, and undeserved, we rage against God or simply withdraw from faith. A natural but self-destructive response is to withdraw from God in anger, demanding from our Creator answers or explanations for the pain. But in our journey through time, we need to acknowledge that our understanding is incomplete, our perspective is limited (1 Cor. 13:12). Although God is capable of withstanding our rage about his poor job performance, ultimately, we must release God from our expectation that he do "our will" and begin to earnestly grapple with our reluctance to do "his will."

If you let go of your anger and bitterness, if you extend forgiveness in humility and seek forgiveness from those you've hurt, you'll begin to walk in new freedom. You'll begin to experience the rewards of a life without bitterness, resentment, and anger. The rewards that might include the medical benefits mentioned by Dr. Swartz above.

But if you're locked in bitterness and anger, how do you cultivate an attitude of forgiveness? Consider these steps:

- Think of a person who's hurt you, someone who makes you seethe with anger when you imagine their face. Take a deep breath and speak forgiveness to that person, out loud. If it has been a long-standing hurt, you may need to repeat your declaration of forgiveness for several days. Your feelings will follow the expression of your will.

- Formulate a one-sentence prayer to whisper each time someone hurts you, such as, *Lord, teach me to forgive them as you've forgiven me.*

- Each day, examine your heart and ask yourself, *Is there anyone I need to forgive or seek forgiveness from today?*

Begin to cultivate a life of forgiveness. The rewards are remarkable. You will live with less anger, less bitterness, and less anxiety. You will begin to hear from God in new ways. Every day, take a few moments to thank God for the ways he has watched over you. His goodness defines our lives, even when the current path is through a deeply shadowed valley.

How Forgiveness Can Change a Direction

After that night with Aunt Mary, I began practicing forgiveness. I made a list of the professors I'd carried a grudge against and spoke forgiveness over them in prayer. Then something unexpected happened within me. I no longer felt trapped in a battle with faculty or admission committees. I had a new freedom to imagine a life without the shadow of defeating my adversaries dominating my thoughts.

There are only a few times I felt God speaking to me near audibly. A few weeks after my trip with Aunt Mary, I was in my dorm room studying. In that room, I heard God say, "You can go." In that moment, I knew just what he meant: that my dream of medical school would materialize. It was a sobering moment. I had sudden clarity, a realization that I had never, not even once, asked God about *his* plans for my life; I had been too busy demanding that he grant me *my* dreams. Still, I wasn't sure I trusted God enough to ask what he wanted for my life. So, quietly, cautiously, I began to pray, *God, is there something you have for me?*

As I explored God's invitations, I considered what might have happened if I hadn't entered into the practice of forgiveness. I would have stayed locked in my bitterness. I would have continued to use it as motivational fuel to pursue a life God didn't want for me. I would have missed God's best for me. And I would have missed my summer in the Philippines. As you'll soon read, it was the summer I learned new lessons about how to cooperate with the Holy Spirit.

AN EXERCISE OF INTENT

1. Here's where it gets real. Spend a few minutes considering people you might need to forgive and write their names in your journal. Imagine their faces in your mind. Imagine how Christ might extend forgiveness to them. Then ask yourself, *How could I hold a grudge when Christ himself offered me his unconditional forgiveness?*

2. Consider the people from whom you need to ask for forgiveness and write their names in your journal. Take steps to make amends.

3. As you move into your one-hundred-day journey of faith, make this agreement with yourself: "When I know I've hurt someone, I will ask for their forgiveness immediately; when someone has hurt me, I will extend forgiveness, whether or not they ask for it."

A PRAYER OF FORGIVENESS

Heavenly Father, give me a forgiving heart, a heart like yours. Teach me to forgive others as you have forgiven me. I release those who have caused me pain and heartache. Forgive me when I hurt others. Create a clean heart within me, a heart that is pleasing in your sight. If there is anything in me separating me from your best, help me to recognize the path to freedom. In Jesus' name, amen.

ELEVEN

INTEND TO WELCOME
THE HOLY SPIRIT

Before the fourteen-hour car ride with Aunt Mary, before the practice of forgiveness unlocked my future, my only goal was to become a doctor. But the truth was, I'd never sought God's wisdom about my future or paused to pray about what he might want for my life. I'd never asked if he wanted me to practice medicine or if he had something else for me. And though I wasn't living a pagan life filled with blatant immorality and debauchery, I was living my own life, making my own plans and setting my own course.

I was a committed believer attending a Christian university, but if I'm honest, I was living the Christian life only out of a sense of duty and responsibility. I thought the great opportunities of life would emerge from my own effort and ability, and if I wanted a full life, it was strictly up to me. In fact, I imagined God would limit my life experiences. I wanted enough faith involvement to avoid hell, but enough distance from God to design my own life dreams and aspirations.

Once I was freed from the bondage of bitterness and resentment, God began to awaken within me a life with new possibilities. I felt a new freedom. I became aware of the opportunity to chart a new course. But I still did not trust God to author my story, so I changed targets. If medical school was not the best destination, surely law school would be a good choice. I had no great love for the law, as I had for medicine, but I liked the lifestyle I thought it would afford. I changed my major, got different advisers, and began to set a new course. All the while I routinely quoted Bible verses at God in an effort to convince him to give me what I wanted. I spoke *at* him, instead of *to* him; I didn't ask for his opinion on the matter. I thought, *Wasn't God supposed to give me the desire of my heart? Wasn't he supposed to bless me, since I was doing all the right things?*

God's patience and persistence are great gifts in our lives. I struggled to understand my future and to graduate on time, which required a focused effort. So I decided that after graduation, a summer mission trip would be an appropriate reward for my four years of hard work. I liked traveling, seeing new places, and meeting new people, and if there was a God-component in the trip, so much the better. I was completely unaware that the Spirit of God was providing counsel in my life. I was just happy the limits had been removed and there were new possibilities before me I had not considered.

I signed up for the university's summer missions program and volunteered for teams traveling to Sweden or Australia. (That's just the kind of man I was, willing to go to the hard places!) But when the time came to receive our assignments, my plans changed.

As we gathered in the auditorium for our assignments, the director addressed the group: "The first group is unique among all the teams we're sending out, because it's a group of only guys, and you are headed to a remote part of the Philippines."

Well, I thought, *I'm glad I'm not going on that trip.*

"We need members in this group who have come from rural backgrounds," he announced.

Hmm, I thought.

"And the group also needs people who have experience doing manual labor."

Uh-oh.

"Finally, we need people who have spent some time around animals."

I didn't really need to hear him announce the names. I knew my summer in Australia was fading fast. As expected, my name was called, and I was headed to the remote island in the Philippines. What I'd originally imagined as more of a vacation than a mission trip had turned into something much more serious. I schemed ways to get out of it. I imagined that if I so much as got a hangnail, I'd bail. But even as I bellyached about the situation, I knew I'd see it through.

I now know that I was taking the next steps at the guidance of the Holy Spirit. He was marking my pathway in spite of me. God was helping me to imagine a new kind of future. Although the changes were often uncomfortable, sometimes awkward, I also had an awareness of opportunity.

God will direct us on some pathways that are not always comfortable or convenient, but he will always lead us toward his best. After all, I had been more than willing to make the sacrifices needed to get into graduate school to achieve my goals. Should I imagine God would require less of me than my professors?

Who Is the Holy Spirit and What Is His Role?

Human beings are complex. The Bible reveals that I am a spirit, I have a soul, and I live in a body. Each part of my person is important to my well-being. In Genesis, we read that we are created in God's image, that God formed Adam from the dust of the ground, and that God breathed into Adam and he became a living being (Gen. 2:7). Our spirit is the part of our person that most directly reflects our Creator, because God is spirit (John 4:24). Growing as a Christ-follower is directly connected to learning to recognize and cooperate with God's Spirit.

Jesus made three statements regarding the person of the Holy Spirit that serve as a wonderful introduction into our lives.

First Statement About the Holy Spirit

Jesus was speaking to his disciples when he made the first statement:

> "But very truly I tell you, it is for your good that I am going away. Unless I go away, the Advocate will not come to you; but if I go, I will send him to you." (John 16:7)

I am confident they thought he was mistaken. After they had invested three years totally committing their lives to following him, he was now saying he was leaving them? And they could not accompany him? This was probably not the bargain they had imagined. They must have felt stifling anxiety. Yet Jesus qualified the promise with "Unless I go away, the Advocate will not come to you."

Let's begin our invitation to the Holy Spirit by accepting Jesus' words that the presence of the Holy Spirit is for *our* good. Jesus made the statement, so we should accept the Holy Spirit without hesitation—no preconditions, no limits, no reluctance. Jesus said he was providing help, so we should intend to cooperate with the Holy Spirit. Every day, I pray the statement: *Holy Spirit, I welcome you into my life today!*

Second Statement About the Holy Spirit

Jesus made a second statement about the Holy Spirit's involvement in our lives:

"But when he, the Spirit of truth, comes, he will guide you into all the truth." (John 16:13)

A guide is a tremendous help. A guide arrives with local knowledge, information, and preparation that we don't have as new arrivals or visitors. A guide makes our efforts more efficient, enabling us to explore opportunities and enjoy resources unknown to outsiders. For example, my brother and I lived in Jerusalem while studying at a Hebrew University some years ago. Many days we would wander the streets, exploring the alleys and shops of the ancient city of Jerusalem. Often, we were just enjoying the journey and had no idea of the historical significance of a location. Since those days, I have led thousands of people on tours to Jerusalem, and some of my closest Israeli friends are tour guides. I have come to understand the tremendous value of a good guide. They know where to get the best food and how to avoid unnecessary interruptions, and they can explain what I am seeing in detail that I cannot duplicate without years of study. In a few days, they helped a tour group more fully experience Israel in ways I had not known as a permanent resident of the city. A guide makes all the difference.

At the heart of Jerusalem is the Old City. It is encircled by a stone wall built in the sixteenth century by Suleiman. Jerusalem has been inhabited for more than three thousand years. King David chose Jerusalem as his capital almost 1,000 BC. There had been many walls built around Jerusalem: King David built a wall. Nehemiah repaired a wall. King Hezekiah built a wall. You can spend countless hours studying the historical record and walking the streets of the Old City, trying to sort out which wall was built by whom and when—or you can have a guide. A good guide already knows the history, the location, and all the frequently asked questions. God has graciously provided us with the help to navigate our journey through time.

Jesus understood this when he said that the Holy Spirit would "guide us into all the truth." I don't imagine his promise to be centered in a more effective Bible study, but rather to be a direction to know God's truth for life.

Jesus said the truth would bring us freedom. In the most significant moments of my life, I have not known what would result in the greatest freedom for me. I lacked the necessary experience or training, even as I was facing decision points. Thus, the promise of a helper who will provide guidance is a tremendous benefit (John 8:32). The Holy Spirit gently guides and directs our lives toward outcomes we don't even know are possible. What we lack, the Spirit of the Creator of all things is present to provide. I have developed the habit of inviting the Holy Spirit for guidance. I often offer a quiet invitation: *Holy Spirit, guide me into the best path. Give me your wisdom.* I am consistently amazed at the outcomes that can only be understood as being a result of God's involvement.

In James 1:5, we are given permission to ask for wisdom. The Holy Spirit is present with us to deliver God's wisdom. It seems foolish to have a guide present who is the designer of the world we live in, has our best interest at heart, and knows what is ahead of us, but not cooperate with him.

I have watched dozens of people on tours ask the guide for direction—what food to try, places to visit on a free day, where to find local artwork for a friend at home—only to listen attentively to the response and then decide to pursue their own ideas. It is not an expression of evil, but they do forfeit the benefit of the guide's knowledge. Cooperating with the Holy Spirit begins with listening, but the benefit arrives when we accept the guidance and choose to walk in obedience to God's direction. Listening to God's counsel is an essential characteristic of God's people throughout Scripture; obedience is our choice to cooperate with the direction provided.

The Holy Spirit will never force compliance; he provides guidance. He is not an authoritarian dictator. We do not have to be afraid of the Holy Spirit embarrassing us or causing us to act in a way beyond the expression of our own will. God has entrusted us with free will. We can choose to listen and obey, or we can reject the counsel of God. An easy way to distinguish between the Holy Spirit and an unholy spirit is by the nature of the invitation. An unholy spirit will dominate, manipulate, and control. I have interacted with many people who have said to me, "I know this behavior is destructive, but I feel powerless to change my actions." They are trapped by an unholy spirit. Only the power of God can set us free from such a predicament.

I have never sat with someone who said, "I don't want to be godly or holy, but I just cannot stop myself." God's Spirit will guide us toward God's best; an unholy spirit will rob you of God's best. You need never fear the presence or activity of the Holy Spirit, because he will guide you into God's very best—even when the path seems contrary to your plans.

Third Statement About the Holy Spirit

The third statement Jesus made regarding the Holy Spirit came after his resurrection. He was preparing the disciples for a life after he left them, a circumstance they were not looking forward to. But once again, Jesus made a complete provision for his friends:

> "But you will receive power when the Holy Spirit comes on you; and you will be my witnesses in Jerusalem, and in all Judea and Samaria, and to the ends of the earth." (Acts 1:8)

Peter, James, John, and the rest of the crew had spent three years with Jesus. They had front-row seats for some of the most remarkable experiences any person could ever witness. They attended water-walking classes, picked up basketfuls of bread from a divinely orchestrated meal of fish and chips, and even sampled a merlot that began as water in a well. Yet Jesus told them they were not ready for the next steps. They needed the assistance of the Holy Spirit, who would empower them to fulfill their life assignments. If the disciples needed the empowering help of the Holy Spirit to complete their life purpose, it seems reasonable that you and I might need to welcome him into our lives as well.

The great barriers to becoming what God created us to be are not physical or financial. The circumstances of our birth, the country that issues our passports, and the name of the school on our diploma are not the great determining factors of our lives. God's power is sufficient to enable us to overcome every limitation that might emerge, even if it is from a destructive expression of evil. But to obtain this freedom, we need the power of God to help us. The Holy Spirit is the delivery person; he is present on the earth to empower us (Jesus' words, not mine).

Our task is not to outthink evil or outwork evil or even outplan evil. The only thing evil will yield to is a power greater than itself. For that victory, we are dependent on the Holy Spirit. What a wonderful promise from Jesus that in his physical absence, he will send the Holy Spirit to empower us to triumphant living! Wherever evil or hate has impacted your life, know for certain that the Spirit of God is present and willing to help you overcome it—and to write an entirely new future for you.

How Cooperation with the Spirit Changed Everything

We arrived at the airport in Manila, and the minute we set foot on Philippine soil, we knew this would be a go-with-the-flow sort of trip. There was no one at the airport to meet us. We waited for hours as a few of us tried to make contact with anyone who could come and get us (a difficult task in the days before cell phones). When we finally got in touch with our hosts, they told us they'd forgotten to tell anyone we were arriving. So we had to find our way to a local hostel and wait there for three days while our transportation to the hosts' island was arranged. When we arrived at the college campus in a remote part of the nation—the place where we were to engage in all that manual labor—there was no agenda or a list of tasks for us to do. There wasn't a leader to direct us either. It seemed as if no one had planned on us being there.

So there we were, a bunch of college kids waiting around for someone to tell us what to do. When it became apparent that it wasn't going to happen, we stopped waiting and began praying and looking for opportunities on our own. We held nightly Bible studies for the college students we were with, we visited hospitals, we went to public schools and performed puppet shows. Wherever we found an open door, we stepped in with some expression of faith. We tried to be available, even when the assignments pulled us into new circumstances. I played basketball in the mornings with the university team.

One afternoon, I was visiting a barrio when I saw a basketball rim (no backboard) tacked onto a palm tree. A kid was shooting hoops with a near-flat basketball, so I went over and rebounded while he continued taking shots. At one point, I caught the ball as it came through the hoop, looked at him, and said, "Dunk?"

He didn't understand, so I rebounded his next shot, took a few steps back, jumped up, and dunked the ball. It hit the ground and rolled toward the boy. He picked up the ball and took off to the village. I thought I must have broken some rule, some cultural tradition, and I half-expected to see a mob running from the village to string me up. But after a few minutes, about three dozen kids followed him out of the brush and stared up at me. The little boy handed me the ball and said, "Dunk?"

I dunked again. Then again. Then again. Those kids asked me to do it again and again, laughing in wonder every time.

I will also never forget the week we spent in the hills on

the island of Panay in the central Visayas. The village where we were staying had no electricity or running water, and the house had been constructed of bamboo and was elevated on poles with the livestock on the ground beneath. We held Bible studies under the stars, praying with people for healing and deliverance who had limited access to medical care of any kind. I was in a place way beyond my comfort zone.

When our stay in this village was over, we hiked a few miles to the nearest road and waited for the local bus to take us back to the closest city. While waiting beside the road, I was hot, tired, and a little grumpy. I thought to myself, *What am I doing? Surely my education and life should be accomplishing more than this.* Out of boredom, I reached into my pack and pulled out my New Testament. It opened to 2 Timothy 1:12: "I know whom I have believed, and am convinced that he is able to guard what I have entrusted to him until that day." I felt like Paul had written the note to me! My days are an investment in God's kingdom; they are not mine to spend casually. Each day is entrusted to God's watchful care. I serve at his pleasure.

After a summer in the Philippines, I returned to Murfreesboro well-tanned and a bit skinnier, but more importantly, with a new awareness of life. I had experienced God outside the walls of traditional church experience. I had seen his provision and direction. I did not yet understand what my future held, but I had the beginning of a new partnership. I was on the way to a life centered in saying yes to the Holy Spirit and a willingness to have my plans redirected. My adventure of saying yes to God was just beginning.

I intend to welcome the Holy Spirit into my life. I am determined to cooperate with him. Religious activity and shallow piety are not sufficient. I am in search of the authentic. Jesus said his departure from earth would make possible something better, the arrival of the Spirit of God. I trust his counsel.

Know this: you will never regret your decision to cooperate with the Holy Spirit.

AN EXERCISE OF INTENT

1. Retrace the years of your life and consider the times the Holy Spirit has intervened. Can you list the specific events and times where God's work was unmistakable? If not, have you ever stopped to invite him to give you direction?

2. In your journal, list the areas of your life where you need a little extra guidance. Maybe you're at a crossroads in your career, you don't know what college major to pursue, or you need help parenting your kids. Write down the specific areas where you're out of your depth, and ask the Holy Spirit to bring his wisdom and guidance to the situation.

3. Ask the Holy Spirit for assistance, and the wisdom to recognize it when it is given. Write down the experience.

A PRAYER TO INVITE THE HOLY SPIRIT

Holy Spirit, I invite you into my life without reservation. Help me learn to recognize the ways you communicate with me. Give me wisdom where I lack it, direction where I'm searching, and help where I need it. Open my eyes to your work and my ears to your words so I may partner with you. In Jesus' name, amen.

TWELVE

INTEND TO CULTIVATE GENEROSITY

A row of Harleys was parked by the church entrance and Steppenwolf blared over a PA system in the parking lot—this was Guy's introduction to World Outreach Church. He'd come with his wife, Clara, who was a regular attender, and though she'd told him about the church, he hadn't expected all this. Not in the least.

Guy had been raised as a Catholic, but had long since given up on the liturgy, the incense, and the communion table. Disappointments and heartaches had left Guy and Clara with a sense of desperation, though. So they decided to try a new church, since nothing else seemed to be working. When Guy stepped into the parking lot on this very different Sunday morning (we don't play "Born to Be Wild" in the church parking lot every week), he paused.

Clara, who knew he was more a skeptic than a believer, asked the next logical question: "Do you want to leave?"

He turned to her, smiling, then said, "No way. I have to see this. Maybe they have a bar in there." (Spoiler alert: we don't.)

World Outreach Church is not a biker church, though we have a few motorcycle enthusiasts who attend. On this Sunday, we'd transformed the church into something that approximated a Harley dealership because I wanted to drive a point home. We even parked a few hogs in the foyer and rolled a couple onto the stage.

Weeks before, I'd read an interview with Jeff Bleustein, the CEO of Harley-Davidson, in which I saw many parallels between motorcycling enthusiasts and the modern church experience. That day I took the podium in a pair of leather chaps and began the sermon by reading snippets from the article. I asked our people to draw the parallels.

In the interview, Bleustein said, "People who are new to motorcycling can find us intimidating . . . they don't know the lingo. They don't know how to get started. We need to lighten our image without losing our edge."[1] Sound familiar? As I walked our congregation through the quotes from the article, Guy listened.

- "Going into a Harley dealership can be intimidating." (Just like going to church.)
- "Harley . . . customers love their bikes—to the point

where they scare off potential customers." (Many avoid Christians, imagining them to be fanatics.)

- "We wanted to take the person who felt like an outsider and turn them into an insider, without insiders feeling as if we were taking away from Harley's image." (The principles of Christianity are timeless, but the delivery system must serve each generation. We have to help the new generation understand the value of God's truth.)
- "Harley dealerships are filled with graybeards and bald heads. We need some young blood in here." (Need I say more?)
- "Harley's appeal straddles class boundaries, stirring the hearts of grease monkeys and corporate titans alike." (Jesus welcomes all who will receive him.)
- "We've changed everything without changing a thing." (Timeless truth delivered in time-sensitive containers.)

I teased out the similarities and said that, as a church, we need to reduce the barriers to entry so those who are curious about the Christian life don't feel like outsiders. I shared how there are certain responses God rewards, and we should cultivate those responses as a people, although we shouldn't expect folks to dive into those practices overnight. For example, we shouldn't act so self-righteous or holier-than-thou. We shouldn't make folks feel like being a good Christian means they have to be perfect or never wrestle with temptation. Instead, I said, we need to invite the curious to explore with us, to cultivate the simple, incremental steps toward deeper faith, even if it means changing our expectations, our language, and our presentation (or that I wear chaps onstage from time to time).

Guy left the service that morning intrigued. He'd later tell me it'd gotten his attention. If he didn't have to have it all together or know all the Christian lingo to be a part of our church, he was free to explore his faith, to get curious. And that's exactly what he did. He began attending church with Clara each week, and later joined a Bible study. As he did, he began to engage the responses that would change his life, such as prayer, intending to grow, honoring God in his home, and working with integrity. Among the most difficult responses, though, was becoming a generous giver.

He never said it outright, but I suspect Guy would describe himself as "a man of large appetites," much the same way Big Dan Teague did in the movie O *Brother, Where Art Thou?*[2] Guy was a salesman. He was a hard worker, a hard player, a hard charger, and a big spender. When he was doing well, he was a big spender; when he wasn't doing so well, he was a pretty big spender too. In fact, by the time he visited the church, he'd made and lost more money than I'll make in a lifetime. He'd declared bankruptcy twice. And though he felt he didn't have a lot of cash to burn when he began exploring the kind of life God rewards, he was curious to see what would happen if he gave sacrificially, something he'd never before considered.

Guy told me on the first Sunday he decided to tithe, his hands shook. As I prayed the prayer before the offering, he pulled out his checkbook and prayed his hand would wither on the spot so he couldn't write the check. No such luck. He scribbled the amount, signed the check, and slipped it into the plate. From this simple act of obedience, something began to shift in his heart.

Generous Living—It's About More Than Money

Cultivating generosity isn't just a good idea; it's an imperative of the Scriptures. And before you assume I'm in league with your pastor or priest, before you assume we're all just trying to get our hands on your bank account, let me assure you that's not the case. Living generously isn't just about money. It's about every facet of your life, every area: the way you spend your time, the way you offer your skills, *and* the way you spend your money. Generosity is a holistic endeavor that flows from the understanding that nothing belongs to you in the first place. Everything you own, every dollar you make, every hour of your time—every bit of it belongs to God.

In Psalm 24:1, the psalmist writes, "The earth is the LORD's, and everything in it, the world, and all who live in it." All material—every speck of gold and silver, every animal, every human—belongs to God. Apart from the material, though, the Bible indicates that time itself belongs to God: "The day is yours, and yours also the night; you established the sun and moon" (Ps. 74:16).

It's true that all material and all time, including our own time, belong to God. And the same is true of all our gifts and talents, all our skills and expertise. In the gospel of Mark, Jesus shared the greatest command:

"'Love the Lord your God with all your heart and with all your soul and with all your mind and with all your strength.' The second is this: 'Love your neighbor as yourself.'" (Mark 12:30–31)

Here, Jesus shares how we should devote every aspect of our being to God, including our gifts, our minds, and our strengths. He then connects using our gifts with loving our neighbors. More than preach it, though, he lived it out. Out of the abundance of his divine wisdom, he offered his time generously to his neighbors, to twelve struggling disciples, to the men and women who needed healing and forgiveness of sins, and ultimately, to a world desperate for a savior.

Generous living is about more than money. It's about all our material, all our time, and all our talents. That said, it's about your pocketbook too. And though you might think it's a tired stereotype—a preacher preaching about money— know this: preachers talk so much about money because the Bible does.

In the Old Testament, God set the parameters around financial giving for his people. In the book of Leviticus, a book laying out the governing law of Israel, the people were to set aside a tithe (10 percent) of everything from the land, "whether grain from the soil or fruit from the trees, belongs to the LORD; it is holy to the LORD" (27:30). As if to remind the people again years later, King Solomon wrote, "Honor the LORD with your wealth, with the firstfruits of all your crops" (Prov. 3:9). And what happened when the people didn't obey the law of the tithe? When they didn't honor God with the firstfruits? The prophets spoke against them. "Will a mere mortal rob God?" Malachi asked. "Yet you rob me. But you ask, 'How are we robbing you?' In tithes and offerings" (Mal. 3:8). But even after this indictment, the prophet delivered the promise of God, a promise that included a blessing:

> "Bring the whole tithe into the storehouse, that there may be food in my house. Test me in this," says the LORD Almighty, "and see if I will not throw open the floodgates of heaven and pour out so much blessing that there will not be room enough to store it." (v. 10)

It's not just the Old Testament texts that speak to the use of money. Jesus preached about money and resources a great deal too, even more than he preached about hell. And though he didn't preach directly about giving a tithe, he preached about giving whatever we had, and he shared the blessings of being a giver. In the book of Matthew, Jesus said, "If anyone gives even a cup of cold water to one of these little ones who is my disciple, truly I tell you, that person will certainly not lose their reward" (10:42). In the gospel of Luke, Jesus said, "Give, and it will be given to you. A good measure, pressed down, shaken together and running over, will be poured into your lap. For with the measure you use, it will be measured to you" (6:38).

It's true that God blesses a generous spirit. But mind this word of caution: Your wealth doesn't indicate whether you've been obedient to God's command to be generous. And conversely, just because you give sacrificially doesn't mean God will make you rich.

Consider the story we all know so well, one about the widow who gave two small copper coins at the temple. Jesus used her as an example of sacrificial giving: "Truly I tell you," he said, "this poor widow has put in more than all the others. All these people gave their gifts out of their wealth; but she out of her poverty put in all she had to live on" (Luke 21:3–4). The most obedient giver was a poor widow. We don't know the rest of the story, and there's no indication that she was blessed with wealth after she gave. Still, my hunch is that God drew close to that poor widow, and he blessed her and provided just what she needed.

God has given us particular gifts: days under the sun, a certain set of talents, particular relationships, various financial resources. These gifts were given to us to steward, to use in loving service to God. So, as we continue to walk this one-hundred-day journey of faith, as we continue to lean into the kind of life God rewards, let's learn to be generous. As you practice more and more generosity, notice how your attitudes shift toward your resources, how you become a better manager of them. Watch, as you begin to be more intentional with your time, giving more of it to those around you. Notice how you forgo impulse purchases as you tend to your money as a resource given by God. And reflect, though I can't explain how this works in God's economy, as you discover that, even if you're not wealthy, you have more than enough.

How Generosity Changes Our Mind-Set

Guy committed himself to tithing, and though I'd like to tell you God showered him with money in response, his transformation was not that simple. Here's what happened: as he tithed, Guy found increasing freedom from his addiction to materialism; he became more disciplined in the ways he spent money; and he experienced great joy in returning a portion of what he'd been given to God. As his view of money changed, he understood he was not defined by possessions. His financial discipline grew, and he became more and more generous, and not just with his money. His changed view of money led to a changed view of time, our most precious resource. He began to give more time to his family, friends, and church. In fact, during the week I was writing this chapter on generosity, he carved out time to help me with a project at the church. For Guy, generosity has become all-encompassing.

Over the years, I've watched Guy give much of his time, expertise, and money. If you asked him, he'd tell you the way he'd managed his resources before he committed his life to God hadn't worked out so well. But after trying God's way, he'd become convinced it was the only way to live. Now, fifteen years later, he's in the middle of the most stable, most productive season of his life. He's more committed, more disciplined, and more intentional. And he's more generous in every facet of his life.

In the same way generosity led Guy to a life of reward, it can lead you there too. Do not allow skepticism to rob you of God's best for your life. Recalibrate the way you handle your resources, and see if what Jesus said is true. Cooperate with God, and don't be surprised when he does what he promises. Don't be surprised when he gives you more than enough.

AN EXERCISE OF INTENT

1. Ask yourself these questions: Am I generous with my time? Do I give sacrificially of it to my family

and friends? What about my talents? Do I use them to point others to Jesus? Do I give financially, at least a tithe to my church? Am I hoarding anything—time, talent, or treasure?

2. After you've answered these questions and identified areas of growth, commit them to the Lord in a one-sentence prayer: *God, lead me to be more generous in sharing my time, talents, and resources.* Incorporate this simple prayer into your daily prayer routine.

3. As you go about your day, particularly as you go about your one-hundred-day journey of faith, look for ways to be more generous. Like Guy, commit to tithe, even if your hand trembles when you write the check. Look for ways to offer a little more time to your spouse, your kids, your friends. Offer to share your gifts with your church, your neighbor, whoever might benefit from them. If you're hoarding something, give it away. Intend to be generous and walk out that generosity in practical ways.

A PRAYER OF GENEROSITY

Heavenly Father, teach me to be a generous person, giving to those in need around me. Give me the discipline to manage resources well, resources you've given me, and help me to return a portion of those resources to you in loving gratitude. Thank you for all you've given me, even the things I take for granted. Give me the courage to share those things with others. In Jesus' name, amen.

THIRTEEN

INTEND TO FINISH WELL

Lee is the businessman's businessman. He climbed the ranks and worked his way through the corporate tangle. He set his sights on success, and after years of hard work and sacrifice, he achieved it, becoming the president of a multinational company. His business acumen wasn't just recognized in his own company, though. He was well-regarded by others in his industry and was invited to serve on the boards of multiple companies. All that success brought a certain kind of lifestyle too: multiple homes, time to enjoy family and friends, and most importantly, the freedom to determine his own schedule.

From the vantage point of most people, Lee was out from under the burden of day-to-day tasks. That made my first meeting with him all the more surprising. I was cycling through the normal questions that emerge when meeting a businessperson with interest in our church, then Lee said,

"My wife and I want something to do. We have no intention of just watching. We are concerned that this church might be too large to need our help, though. Are there things we can do?" Wow. Most high-powered, accomplished folks arrive ready to tell others what to do, not roll up their sleeves and ask to step into the fray.

A few years ago, Lee retired from the day-to-day responsibilities of his job. And though he could have spent his retirement years doing whatever he wanted, wherever he wanted—Colorado, the Hamptons, the Swiss Alps—he preferred a different path: he chose to use his business skills, his influence, and his faith to coach those coming up behind him.

These days, Lee spends his time with businesspeople who need a little help. He walks with the men and women in our church and community through their particular business conundrum, whether they need to hone their leadership skills, their business models, or their financial wherewithal. With skill and patience, he helps them overcome roadblocks and move toward success. But he doesn't just help businesspeople. He's spent countless hours helping me think through projects, opportunities, and problem areas at the church. And by working closely with Lee, I've learned so much about leadership.

Lee is an example of someone who looks to finish well in every phase of life. He finished well in his career, and as he's entered a new season, he has set his sights on finishing well in that too. Perhaps this is exactly what you'd imagine when you hear the phrase *finish well*: a retiree beginning a new season of life with the same sense of sacrifice and focus that enabled his earlier successes. But no matter what season of life you are in, no matter what task you have before you, you have an opportunity to finish well.

Consider Abby, a young lady who'd been attending our church. I first met her when she was wrapping up junior high school. A friend had invited her to our youth group, where she began a journey of faith. Raised in an unreligious home, she'd been coming to church on her own and doing her best to learn all she could about aligning her life with the heart of God. I watched her mature as a young person, a student, and a Christ-follower. She had a unique heart for God. Her life was not always easy; she grew up with limited resources and other obstacles. But she was exceptionally bright and creative, marched to the beat of her own drum, *and* displayed an intent to honor God.

Abby graduated from high school with honors and received a scholarship to college. She set her sights on finishing well in college too. Over the next handful of years, she earned multiple degrees, was an advocate for godly living, and met and married the kind of guy any parent would be proud to call a son-in-law. Abby had learned to flourish in junior high school, and she continued flourishing well into her adulthood. Why? She understood the power of endurance, of finishing every season well. And as a result, she's had great impact on the world around her. In fact, her dad now plays music in our church worship band.

From Lee and Abby, we learn that it doesn't matter where you are on life's spectrum, whether in your teens or in your sixties. It doesn't matter whether you're in school, in your working years, or in retirement. Every season provides an opportunity to live a life of intentional faith.

I had a breakthrough in my understanding about life. My life is not a single event with a beginning and an end; my life is a collection of seasons and stories. I have had multiple beginnings, and I look forward to multiple endings. I know from Scripture we take only one trip through time, but our lives are filled with times and seasons, as the author of Ecclesiastes reminds us. Each of those seasons provides a new beginning and an opportunity to finish well. The momentum from each season I finish well propels me toward God's best in the next season.

The Power of Perseverance

We love convenient solutions. The quick and easy stuff. If you need an answer, google it. When Christmas season comes around, pull out your cell phone and have the presents sent to your door with one click. Need to be in New York by tomorrow? Book a flight with the push of a button. Everything is immediate—instant pudding, instant oatmeal, instant abs. We want everything now, and sometimes even faster.

In this age of instant gratification and digital convenience, we've suffered. An oft-quoted *Time* magazine article reports:

> The average attention span for the notoriously ill-focused goldfish is nine seconds, but according to a new study from Microsoft Corp., people now generally lose concentration after eight seconds, highlighting the effects of an increasingly digitalized lifestyle on the brain.[1]

We are neurologically devolving. Our collective attention span is taking its rightful place somewhere between the gnat and the goldfish. Does that get your attention?

When it comes to the best things in life, there are no quick fixes. Good things take time, focused attention, and a commitment to finish. Gourmet chefs don't microwave their finest meals. Elite athletes don't become finely tuned machines overnight. Raising good kids requires years of patient instruction, discipline, and presence. Becoming skilled in your vocation requires long dedication to excellence, respecting coworkers, and working as unto the Lord. Staying in shape requires putting in the hours at the gym, cultivating a long-term healthy lifestyle, and a commitment to maintaining that routine, even when no one is watching. Everything worth having in life requires commitment to a task, perseverance to complete it, and dedication to do it well. Is the spiritual life any different?

It should come as no surprise that in the Bible, faith and perseverance are linked. A healthy spiritual life is not the outcome of an emotional moment or a breakthrough idea. The path of a Christ-follower is filled with many junctions where decisions are processed, and honoring God is the determined objective. Oftentimes the process is halting, our momentum broken by our failures or the failures of others. But, in the midst of the journey, the grace and mercy of God provide the momentum for progress.

Our biblical heroes understood the power of perseverance. Consider Joseph, who was sold into slavery by his brothers and found himself working as a servant in the house of Potiphar, an Egyptian nobleman. When Potiphar's wife tried to seduce him, Joseph refused. He told her he was devoted to his master and God, and asked, "How then could I do such a wicked thing and sin against God?" (Gen. 39:9). What did Joseph get for his commitment to follow God? A false accusation of attempted rape, an unjust conviction, and a long-term imprisonment.

Prison. Certainly not an assignment from the Lord any of us would want. But while in prison, Joseph persevered, and as a result, became known as a model prisoner. Intending to finish his prison sentence well, he gained favor with the warden, who put him in charge of the other prisoners and "paid no attention to anything under Joseph's care, because the LORD was with Joseph and gave him success in whatever he did" (v. 23).

After two years in prison, Joseph again found favor through a series of dream interpretations and was promoted to the king's court, where he became the manager of all the pharaoh's resources. And again, Joseph continued to honor the Lord in the task. By his commitment to the season before him, Joseph prepared the country for the coming famine; when that famine hit, he'd stored more than enough grain to feed the people of Egypt and the surrounding country. And when his brothers (the same ones who'd sold him into slavery) made the trek to Egypt in search of food, Joseph was able to provide for them. No matter the task before him, Joseph intended to carry it to completion—to finish well.

The same is true for so many biblical characters. Moses had been called to lead the Israelites to freedom from Egyptian slavery, an impossible task, and one that required perseverance to finish well. He wrangled with Pharaoh for months, enduring ten plagues to procure the release of the Israelites. But after leading the people out of Egypt, Moses was faced with another, more arduous task: fashioning a nation from a mixed multitude of people who had never known independence. God intervened in miraculous ways, with consistent supernatural affirmation of Moses and his leadership: he provided the Ten Commandments, pillars of cloud and fire, manna, even water from a rock in the desert. Yet the people frequently grumbled about Moses' leadership and the difficulty of the path they were on. Due to their complaints against God, the journey that was intended to be for a few months became a forty-year assignment. Moses' decision to honor God was not grounded in Pharaoh's compliance or the Hebrew people's appreciation; he understood the objective was a life offered to God. With each challenge, Moses chose to finish well.

And let's consider Jesus, our perfect example of commitment to persevering to the end and finishing well.

Let us run with perseverance the race marked out for us, fixing our eyes on Jesus, the pioneer and perfecter of faith. For the joy set before him he endured the cross, scorning its shame, and sat down at the right hand of the throne of God. Consider him who endured such opposition from sinners, so that you will not grow weary and lose heart. In your struggle against sin, you have not yet resisted to the point of shedding your blood. (Heb. 12:1–4)

The path Jesus was asked to walk included some pretty difficult seasons. He walked through the shame of rejection, the false accusation, and the humiliation of execution. He endured opposition from sinful, evil people. We are asked to reflect upon Jesus' assignment, so that we will not yield to the demands of weariness. Exhaustion asks us to quit, to surrender, yet we are encouraged to acknowledge the struggle but not to yield. Jesus is our example of this, and the one who is now interceding on our behalf. We are not alone, even when an ally or a word of encouragement is absent. Jesus is watching over us, and he understands our challenges. He is our deliverer.

Finishing Well–It's More Than a One-Time Decision

Like Joseph, Moses, and Jesus, we've been given particular tasks, assignments, and seasons. As the writer of Hebrews puts it, we've been called to "run with perseverance the race marked out for us" (12:1). We can either commit to those tasks and seasons or give up and quit.

The apostle Paul reminds us of the reward for finishing well:

I have fought the good fight, I have finished the race, I have kept the faith. Now there is in store for me the crown of righteousness, which the Lord, the righteous Judge, will award to me on that day—and not only to me, but also to all who have longed for his appearing. (2 Tim. 4:7–8)

Paul was aware that his death was imminent, but he was not despondent. Quite the opposite. He was filled with anticipation for the crown of righteousness! The best news is that it is not a singular award for the apostle. It is available for all of us who persevere and finish our course in anticipation of seeing our Lord.

As we've seen in this book, experiencing connection with God is not about making a one-time decision, praying a prayer, or being dunked in a baptismal pool (though those are all good things). Connecting with God, pursuing a life he rewards, is a marathon, not a sprint. We commit to grow, to pray, and to read the Bible, no matter what season of life we're in. We commit to honor God in our home, to work with integrity, and to teach the younger generation. We commit to forgive, to participate with the Holy Spirit, and to live generously. And we commit to finish well.

If you're a high school or college student, commit to finishing your scholastic season honoring the Lord.

If you're a businessperson, persevere in doing good, intending to finish that season well.

If you're a stay-at-home mom or a corporate achiever, finish your season in a way that leaves no doubt about your faithful service to our Lord.

Persevere. Complete your task well. If you do, you'll discover the satisfaction and joys of a race well run. But they aren't all you'll experience. In Revelation, the closing book of the Bible, God shares this promise for those who complete their assignment well: "To the one who is victorious, I will give the right to eat from the tree of life, which is in the paradise of God" (2:7). And in its final chapter, he shares the ultimate reward:

"Look! God's dwelling place is now among the people, and he will dwell with them. They will be his people, and God himself will be with them and be their God. 'He will wipe every tear from their eyes. There will be no more death' or mourning or crying or pain, for the old order of things has passed away." (21:3–4)

If you've picked up this book in a season when the demands are great and the finish line is not visible, I want to remind you that God has promised rest. Even God rested from his work on the seventh day. Refreshing is a gift from the Lord; rest is necessary to complete your assignment. Ask God to provide the rest and renewal needed to complete the course. God knows how to give them to you—ask him. Sometimes he'll give you a word from the Scriptures or a line from a song that brings renewed hope. Sometimes he may just give you a space to sit in the quiet and recharge. Just remember, weariness and fatigue are not indicators of failure. Quite the opposite. They signify effort. Don't give up, and set your sights on finishing well!

Finish Each Season Well

Every season of life comes with its own struggles, assignments, and opportunities. It comes with its own tasks, too, and sometimes those tasks aren't the things we'd rather be doing. Like Joseph, you might be tasked with an assignment most would decline, something akin to servanthood or even involuntary incarceration. Like Moses, you might be tasked to lead a group of grumbling and ungrateful people. And like Jesus, maybe you'll suffer indignity and persecution as you walk out your faith. No matter the situation, though, remember that you've been given an important assignment by God in an important season of your life. Set out to finish well.

Sandra set out to do just that. She is a lot like Lee. She looks like the quintessential portrait of the American success story. She is an attorney with a busy practice, and she has a lengthy list of accomplishments in her profession, community service, and personal life. She has also had to overcome a great deal: cancer, the loss of a husband, the ups and downs of a business. If she were anything like so many of us in the world today, she'd slow down. She doesn't, though. Instead, she pays attention to the work of God in the world around her and joins him in it. You'll find her leading small-group Bible studies during the week or volunteering in the nursery. You'll find her pouring into the younger generation. One thing is for sure, you'll find Sandra about the work of the kingdom.

Sandra is finishing well, and she's leading others to do the same. She leads a small group in her home, complete with dinner each week. (I volunteer to teach there just because of the culinary opportunity.) It is a diverse group of men and women, young and old, sophisticated and simple—all are welcomed and treated with dignity. I know a young, single woman who attends, and if you ask her why, she'll tell you she enjoys being around Sandra and gleaning from her lifetime of wisdom. When I asked what most impressed her about Sandra, she said, "She always prays to finish well." And this prayer encouraged the young woman to finish her season of singleness well too.

The followers of Christ are in a relay race together. Some of us are in the first leg of our journey with God, while others are in the homestretch. No matter your position, though, don't give up. You've been called to finish this season well, serving as an example for the one to whom you'll hand the baton.

I intend for the best days to be the days ahead. I refuse to allow my story to be understood by a recitation of past activity, whether achievement or failure. I am happy for those who dream dreams of what was, but I choose to live with a vision of what can be. I am not striving for a participation trophy. I realize the finish line is the point of evaluation, and all that precedes it is just preparation. I have offered myself in service to the King of kings, and I intend to be about his business until the moment he steps into time or I step out.

So wherever you are in years, in your career, or even in this simple commitment to a one-hundred-day journey of faith, persevere and experience the rewards that come with finishing well. You will never regret giving your best to honor our Lord!

AN EXERCISE OF INTENT

1. Consider the various seasons of your life—high school, college, parenthood, your last job. Did you pursue God all the way to the end? If not, make a list in your journal of the reasons why you didn't.
2. Think about the season you're currently in. Write down some particular ways you can engage the practices written in this book so you can persevere.
3. Identify a person or two in your life who can keep you accountable to finishing your current season well. Write down their names, then take the steps necessary to invite them to walk with you through this season.

A PRAYER FOR PERSEVERANCE

Heavenly Father, give me the strength to persevere in this season of my life. Help me to do what it takes to connect with you daily, to respond to you in all that I do, and to participate with you in bringing life to the world around me. Allow me to finish well. In Jesus' name, amen.

PART FIVE

INTENTIONAL FAITH: AN INVITATION TO KINGDOM IMPACT

Your kingdom come,
your will be done,
    on earth as it is in heaven.

—Matthew 6:10

When we live completely committed lives of intentional faith, when we align our hearts with the heart of God, amazing things happen. We begin to receive the rewards of a God-oriented life. Our life outcomes change, and we carry the kingdom into the world. Learn how that kind of faith will change you and the world.

FOURTEEN

CHANGED LIVES, CHANGED COMMUNITIES

I met Mike when I was thirteen and we were on the same basketball team in junior high school. In many ways we were opposites, but in the most important ways, we were very much the same. We both loved to play basketball. Whereas he was a naturally gifted athlete with an intense desire to compete, I was a pretty average athlete without the good sense to quit. I understood my limits and appreciated his talent. Mike was not just a gifted athlete, though; he had a gift for making people feel valuable. He had a smile that radiated and a heart of compassion for people that was expressed through his whole countenance. These characteristics were true when he was a boy and became even more evident as he grew into a man.

As boys playing basketball, our lives were centered on competition through junior and senior years. It wasn't until many years later that I learned more about my friend's childhood. I knew his family circumstances were difficult. He was being raised by his grandmother and was essentially on his own. He had a place to sleep but not really much direction in his life. When we could drive, he never wanted me to drop him off at home after practice or a game, but I was too young or immature to consider why.

We lost touch for a few years when I left Tennessee to attend college in Oklahoma, but we reconnected when I returned to Murfreesboro. Mike had a beautiful wife and was working hard to make life work. But the gravitational pull of his past was pushing him into some destructive places. Hard work and determination were not enough; he needed the power of God to bring restoration. At the time I was learning what it meant to be a pastor, so I was a witness to God changing both our lives. I saw God bring healing and deliverance from the hurt and rejection that had been so much a part of Mike's early life.

A community of faith is a powerful thing. Life together with friends and families, all walking a path of faith with a desire to honor the Lord, provides a climate for spiritual change. The gentle direction of the Holy Spirit identifies the places where our stubborn refusal to cooperate puts unnecessary limits on our lives. The same things that made Mike and me successful on the basketball court—a refusal to quit, a strong sense of self, and an indomitable will—we now had to learn to yield to God and others.

Just as we had trained for athletics, God put us in training for his kingdom. Mike became a pillar in our congregation. He was a leader of leaders, and his broad smile belied his great strength. I learned a lesson from observing him that I have never forgotten: gentleness is an expression of strength, not weakness. Mike's big smile and friendly demeanor extended from his strength of body and character. And because he had suffered greatly, he had compassion for people who were walking a difficult path.

How God Uses a Changed Life

I have come to the conclusion that growing churches are comprised of growing people. For our communities of faith—or communities of any kind—to flourish, change directed by the lordship of Jesus of Nazareth is essential. The most powerful part of the process is the transformation of a life.

The emphasis on personal salvation has had some negative impacts on the development of our faith. I believe in personal salvation, conversion, being born-again, whichever label for initiation into the kingdom of God you prefer. Our journeys begin with a very personal decision about the person of Jesus Christ and choosing him as our Lord. However, our growth and maturity are linked to community and life together. The New Testament uses the imagery of a body, with each part being interdependent. No single part can flourish without the support and vitality of the other parts of the body. The awkward truth of our faith is that we need one another in order to fulfill what God has created us for. The objective is not about doing big things for God but learning to be faithful in the often-overlooked places of faithfulness and friendship, with God and one another.

Some years after I reconnected with Mike, God brought another man into our congregation with some new lessons to share. I met Charles on the first Sunday he visited our church. He said a friend had invited him, and although he didn't want to attend, he also didn't want to offend his friend. He would later tell me his goal was to be so disrespectful to people at church that he would be rejected, giving him a good reason to back out if his friend invited him again. On that first Sunday, he tested our boundaries. He wore cutoff shorts, got high before he came, and then sat on the front row so he could not be overlooked.

By this time I had been serving in church a few years, so I had a little more experience in dealing with people like Charles. I had also expressed enough rebellion in my life to recognize a fellow traveler. Charles looked to me like the kind of character God would choose to use for his work in the world. He continued attending church, always expecting to be shown the door, and we eventually struck up a friendship. He'd invite me to attend a Titans game or grab lunch.

Layer by layer, Charles began to choose to honor the Lord. He made new friends, picked up some healthier hobbies, and later came to work at the church. His assignment was to keep our expanding facilities in pristine condition, and he took to the task with the focused intensity of a neurosurgeon.

As our friendship grew, Charles shared more about his childhood and early life, which had been disastrous. His parents had not really been prepared for the two sons they were entrusted with. On one occasion, Charles came home from elementary school to find his parents had moved without telling anyone where they went, including him and his brother. He was smiling as he told me the story. It was obvious God had brought some tremendous deliverance and healing into his life.

Charles understood what it felt like to be rejected and alone, and when he discovered the healing grace of Jesus of Nazareth, he was all in. The unexpected reward was how God used Charles's painful circumstances to become a strength to so many people. He had a humility that allowed him to interact with anyone, and he befriended many throughout the church. He would cook delicious barbecue for friends, which included a lengthy discussion about the best sauces and temperatures (the result was usually worth the listening). Over the years, I've witnessed dozens and dozens of people call on Charles whenever there was a crisis, and he'd always step into the circumstance and become a part of the solution. Some who called were powerful, highly successful businessmen, and others were struggling with addiction and life at the bottom. Regardless of who they were, Charles would offer his help without criticism or judgment, because he understood the power of God's truth to change a life and write a new future.

Present Circumstances Do Not Dictate Your Future

I learned life-changing lessons from my friends Mike and Charles: the circumstances of our birth do not have the power to dictate our future if we are connected to God. I, too, have experienced the power of healing from rejection and suffering. And I have seen the strength of God delivered in ways that enable others to change for themselves.

Changed lives and changed communities are two sides of the same coin. Growing churches are comprised of growing people. It is not architecture, budgets, or theological statements that transform lives. Men and women learning to yield to God and allowing him to bring wholeness to their lives is the heart of faith. No one is beyond the grace of God, and no one is above the need of the redemptive work of Jesus of Nazareth.

When I look at the congregation of World Outreach Church today, I realize we are more of a hospital for those being restored to spiritual wholeness than we are a hall of fame of spiritual accomplishment. Our lives are the canvas upon which the mercy and power of God are displayed. Our brokenness and failure did not disqualify us from participation; rather, it nominated us for special service. God is faithful to restore and renew our lives if we choose to walk toward him each day. His desire to help us is far greater than our desire to seek him. God is faithful. You can trust him.

Jesus' Call into Kingdom Community

In the book of Acts, Luke, the doctor-turned-Jesus-storyteller, records how the Holy Spirit used changed lives to give birth to a changed community. In the second chapter, we find the disciples gathered in an upstairs room after Jesus' death, resurrection, and ascension. There, the Holy Spirit fell on them and, filled with his power, they made their way to the streets of Jerusalem and began preaching the message of Jesus to the masses. What was the result? Over three thousand people followed Christ and began walking out their own stories of intentional faith.

This new community of faith was unlike anything the world had to offer. Luke, a participant in that community, wrote:

> They devoted themselves to the apostles' teaching and to fellowship, to the breaking of bread and to prayer. Everyone was filled with awe at the many wonders and signs performed by the apostles. All the believers were together and had everything in common. They

sold property and possessions to give to anyone who had need. Every day they continued to meet together in the temple courts. They broke bread in their homes and ate together with glad and sincere hearts, praising God and enjoying the favor of all the people. And the Lord added to their number daily those who were being saved. (Acts 2:42–47)

From the very beginning, Christ intended that changed lives would come together to form a different kind of community, one that wasn't defined by some highly individualistic private philosophy of salvation. Instead, it was to be a community that was devoted and generous, and took care of one another; a community of praise; and a community that served as an example of the kingdom of God on earth. And did it ever.

- The lame were healed (Acts 3:1–10).
- The paralyzed were made whole (Acts 9:32–35).
- A woman was restored to life (Acts 9:36–41).
- Demons were cast out (Acts 16:16–18).

Throughout the New Testament, the members of that early community teach us that our Christian lives aren't meant to be lived out in isolation but in kingdom community. In 1 Corinthians 12, Paul reminds us that we do not live lives of isolated faith, and that the entire community of faith comprises one body (v. 27). In Romans, Paul again writes that "in Christ we, though many, form one body, and each member belongs to all the others" (12:5). In 1 Peter, the disciple and friend of Jesus writes, "Each of you should use whatever gift you have received to serve others, as faithful stewards of God's grace" (4:10). In the book of James, we're instructed to "confess your sins to each other and pray for each other" (5:16), an admonition that requires participation in a broader community.

Jesus is the same yesterday, today, and forever. But for us, change is mandatory if we intend to grow. The journey of being a Christ-follower is about being changed by Jesus. He is actively helping people find freedom and purpose. He is awaiting our response!

AN EXERCISE OF INTENT

1. How are you engaged in the community of change, the church? Are you an active participant?

2. How does your church impact the world around it? If it doesn't, why not?

3. What are some ways you can encourage others in your community to join you in the pursuit of expressing an intentional faith? If you are going through the one-hundred-day season of faith, write down your experience in a journal so you can remind yourself of the journey later.

A PRAYER FOR TRANSFORMATION

Almighty God, only you are able to bring wholeness into my life. I yield to your direction and truth. Open my heart to your Word. Lead me in paths of righteousness. Establish me in the security of your strength. Deliver me from every temptation, and restore the places devastated by ungodliness. I trust you with my future. In Jesus' name, amen.

FIFTEEN

THE POWER OF A SEASON

It has been ten years since I faced the awkward and embarrassing reality that I was *obese* (the doctor's term, not mine). I preferred to think of myself as having a more mature physique. So when I went to the doctor, a friend, for a routine physical and he said, "Allen, if you don't lose some weight, I will have to classify you as obese," I was offended, and certain a new doctor was my solution.

I left his office intending to hunt down a second opinion, but in an inspired moment of clarity, I knew he was right. I had always been active and athletic, participating in team sports and manual labor, so how could I have arrived at this place? I knew exactly how: one casual snack at a time; one extra dessert at a time. I decided change was necessary. I bought new workout clothes and new running shoes. I tried them on and looked healthier already. When I had time and it was convenient, I began jogging, but otherwise, not much changed.

Though I wasn't trimming up (turns out an occasional jog doesn't mean you can eat an extra pie), I was experiencing success in other areas. The church I served was growing. We needed to add another weekend worship service—number four—because adding a service was more efficient than building larger spaces. Our ministry teams were doing well. And with so many things going on at the church, I didn't have the energy to add another assignment to my weekend schedule.

Months passed and nothing changed; I felt miserable. I knew I had to consider my health again. But this time I chose a new course. I wasn't going to simply nurse a private commitment to exercise a bit more and curtail my dessert consumption; instead, I was going to ask for help.

I went to the gym and hired a personal trainer. Like with the doctor, it was awkward and a bit embarrassing, and for the first few weeks, painful. I will never forget my first physical evaluation. In the middle of a gym, filled with people I happened to know, the trainer ran me through a series of exercises that made it abundantly clear how indulgent my lifestyle had become. I had earned multiple degrees, achieved a fair amount of professional success, and traveled around the world, yet I was struggling to do sit-ups and push-ups and run on a treadmill. I was floundering in basic health.

The trainer reminded me of what I already knew: the only way to gain new strength is to exercise to the point of fatigue and muscle failure. Day after day, I found myself in the gym, failing—in public—under the tutelage of a twenty-year-old who didn't yet understand the humility aging brings to our physical abilities. Nevertheless, I persevered. Days, weeks, and months passed. I brought my diet under scrutiny and made new choices, new habits, new routines. Finally, I lost fifty pounds, found a whole new energy for life assignments, and learned afresh the power of incremental change.

The most challenging part of the journey was the realization that I could not orchestrate the change I wanted in a day of frenzied effort or even a week of focused response. Instead, I was faced with the privilege of engaging in a set of behaviors that would bring a dramatic new opportunity. Through small steps, sore muscles, and new "favorite" foods, a new set of possibilities emerged.

As the winter slogged on, I found myself adjusting my life to make sure I wouldn't disrupt the new rhythm that was emerging. I didn't stay up too late to read or watch football. I ate the things that would give me energy for my workouts. And that spring, by the time the daffodils pushed up in Murfreesboro, I'd lost weight, felt better, and looked forward to my morning exercise. Day by day, incrementally, my season of commitment led to the outcome I wanted.

That's the power of a season. It can lead to new rhythms and changed habits. And commitments to spiritual seasons are no different. When we commit to connect with God, even if it just starts with a short season, we develop habits that train our spiritual hearts. Through daily expressions of our faith, incrementally, we find our hearts beating in rhythm with God's.

Setting a Spiritual Heart Rhythm

Have you considered how important the rhythm of your heart is? When your heart beats arrhythmically, it can lead to fatigue, weakness, or even death. In the same way, it's possible for your spiritual heart to weaken, beat off cadence, and be out of rhythm with God's heart. How? Your heart might beat to your own rhythm as you chase passions that are misdirected, unhealthy, and even dangerous. You can follow what's natural, emotional, or even logical, and find yourself still coming up empty. But by developing habits that connect you with God's Spirit, by syncing your heartbeat with his, you'll find new meaning and purpose.

Let me be clear: it won't be easy to develop new spiritual habits, at least not at first. In fact, you'll be met with your own resistance, and you'll face unexpected challenges as you train toward godliness. How do I know? Because Scripture promises life is full of unexpected, ever-changing seasons. Take Ecclesiastes 3:1–4, for example:

> There is a time for everything,
>> and a season for every activity under the heavens:
>> a time to be born and a time to die,

> a time to plant and a time to uproot,
>
> a time to kill and a time to heal,
>
> a time to tear down and a time to build,
>
> a time to weep and a time to laugh,
>
> a time to mourn and a time to dance.

If I were writing Scripture, I would change this passage. I would take out "a time to die," "a time to uproot," "a time to tear down," "a time to weep," and "a time to mourn." I do not like those seasons nearly as much as I enjoy seasons of laughter and building. But our reality is that life is filled with changes we did not anticipate or schedule. We are constantly moving from seasons of ease to seasons of distress, from seasons of joy to seasons of pain, from this experience to that experience. We don't swim in one unending, blissful stream of ease.

Choosing to follow the Lord intentionally will not eliminate the unwanted seasons from your life. It can, however, prepare you to respond in a new way—from a place of strength and faith. Involvement with God puts our hearts in sync with his, and it will change the outputs of our lives. What will the result be?

If we develop habits that keep our spiritual hearts healthy, we'll have the power to respond in supernatural ways, no matter what life throws in our path. Consider our most perfect example: Jesus. Recall his last moments on the cross. He'd been tried unfairly, stripped, whipped, beaten, humiliated, and disgraced. He had a crown of thorns pounded onto his head and was forced to carry the cross he would eventually die on. Everything he'd experienced, everything he'd been put through, should have led him to anger and bitterness. But at the height of his pain and humiliation, crucified on a cross between two thieves, he didn't call down curses on the people who were murdering him. He didn't cry out to God for retribution. What was his response in that season of pain and humiliation? What did he say when he barely had the strength to speak?

"Father, forgive them, for they do not know what they are doing." (Luke 23:34)

He forgave them, even in the face of pain and torture and slander and humiliation. It was not a natural response. It was not a logical response. It was not the type of forgiveness that wells up inside any of us automatically. Jesus had the power to forgive because he'd spent a lifetime practicing habits of godliness, keeping his heart in rhythm with the heart of God. Jesus understood something: his obedience and cooperation with God would bring a reward that far exceeded the momentary affliction. And so he endured.

Consider how Paul put it in his letter to the Philippians:

He humbled himself
by becoming obedient to death—

> even death on a cross!
> Therefore God exalted him to the highest place
> and gave him the name that is above every name.
>
> (2:8–9)

The Power of One Hundred Days of Faith

A single season has the power to change the trajectory of the rest of your life.

When it comes to the many seasons we experience in our lives, we often have no choice in the matter. We don't ask for cancer. We don't ask for the unexpected severance package. We don't ask for the death of a loved one. We don't have a say in when we will experience the winter seasons in our lives: the mourning, the dying, the tearing down. And though we don't have the power to avoid these seasons, we have the power to cultivate habits that lead us to better outcomes during these seasons. I want to invite you to choose to have a season of cultivating these habits.

In the next chapter, I'm going to ask you to make a commitment to a one-hundred-day season of intentionally applying the daily habits and life choices laid out in this book. For the skeptics in the room, you might believe that a hundred days isn't enough time to develop new spiritual habits, that charting a new spiritual course takes more time. But consider the power of one hundred days. Political scientists and historians tell us that the first hundred days of a presidency sets the tone for the entire term of office; and if you look back, this has proven to be true. Biologists and pediatricians tell us that the first one hundred days in the womb are as important for the overall development of the baby's physical health as any one-hundred-day window in their entire life. And a simple Google search will show just how many people have used one-hundred-day time frames to develop better, healthier eating and exercise habits.

A one-hundred-day commitment can be transformational in so many areas of life, and the same can be true of your spiritual life. Just as my commitment to health led to changed outcomes—weight loss, increased energy, better-fitting suits—your one-hundred-day commitment to faith will result in changed outcomes too. You'll find yourself with more peace and endurance during difficult seasons. You'll find more purpose in everyday living. You'll be more loving, more understanding, and, like Jesus, more forgiving. In short, you'll live a life that's more connected with God.

AN EXERCISE OF INTENT

1. Consider a time in your life when you changed your habits to achieve better physical, emotional, or spiritual health. How long did it take you to see results?

2. In your journal, make a list of things that you feel may get in the way of your committing to a season of intentionally seeking God, such as fears, time constraints, negative influences, and so on. Then ask the Lord in prayer for help to overcome these barriers.

3. Plan and gather anything you might need to be ready for this intentional season. Consider noting daily time on your calendar to pray or to read the Bible. Maybe you need to purchase a new Bible or a journal. You may even want to ask a friend or a family member to be your accountability partner.

A PRAYER FOR A NEW SEASON

Heavenly Father, give me the strength to commit to this season of focused intention. Give me endurance and stamina as I pursue you, as I respond to your calling. Allow me to notice the changes you're making in my life, the rewards you're giving me in these one hundred days, and help me to continue to press into the season. Amen.

SIXTEEN

AN INVITATION TO ONE HUNDRED DAYS OF FAITH

M y objective as a pastor is not to deliver religious lectures. My goal is to initiate movement toward the Lord.

You may have a long history of faith and faithfulness, or you may be just beginning a relationship with God. Either way, the ten ideas that you've read about in this book are essential to thrive as a Christ-follower. Remember how simple they are in theory but how profound they can be in practice. It's interesting that practicing them can sometimes be more about heart attitude and intent than a list of to-dos. Admittedly, reading your Bible will take a few minutes, but without spiritual nourishment, there is no hope of gaining new strength.

Take a minute to review the ten ideas outlined in this book that will be your focus if you choose to commit to one hundred days of faith:

1. Intend to grow
2. Intend to read the New Testament
3. Intend to pray
4. Intend to honor God in your home
5. Intend to work with integrity
6. Intend to teach the younger generation
7. Intend to practice forgiveness
8. Intend to welcome the Holy Spirit
9. Intend to cultivate generosity
10. Intend to finish well

I like seeing these expressions of faith together like this, because they are meant to be used as components of one effort. They aren't à la carte menu items or workout routines for you to pick and choose from. Just as you would create an exercise plan that incorporates your whole body to remain physically healthy, you should follow a spiritual plan that encompasses every aspect of your life. You could choose to pick up only one or two of the easiest expressions of faith listed, but that kind of pick-and-choose spirituality won't lead you into a deeper connection with God. Think about it: If you pray and read the Scriptures to the exclusion of honoring God in your home, what good was all that praying and reading?

If you are weary and frustrated with faith, and maybe even with the *people* of faith, just remember from my gym experience that the only way to gain physical strength is to exercise to the point of fatigue. Without exercise, your muscles atrophy. If you are spiritually and emotionally fatigued, it is not a sign of failure or inadequacy but a symptom of spiritual and emotional exercise. You are in the process of gaining new strength.

I also don't want you to think of these spiritual practices as more to-dos to add to your already busy list of life responsibilities, because they can become simple habits of faith once they are established. They will not add more burden to your life; instead, they will replace your old responses to life in a way that allows you to live a life God rewards.

Maybe all this sounds too good to be true. Maybe it sounds too simplistic or unsophisticated. Maybe you don't think it'll work for you or don't think it's doable. That's fine. Then perhaps do it as a challenge just to prove me wrong. On the other hand, maybe this sounds exactly like what you've been waiting for: an opportunity to experience God in a new way. If so, come along. That's just what you'll find when you join me in these one hundred days.

As I mentioned at the beginning of this chapter, my objective as a pastor isn't to deliver religious lectures; it's to help people initiate movement toward the Lord. This book is not intended merely to inform or educate but to extend a personal invitation. Whatever your spiritual journey has been up to this point, now is the time to establish yourself in a new place of powerful alignment with God.

I'm inviting you to go on a journey that will unfold as you embrace the ten fundamentals of this book. It's a season of focused spiritual training and action to *grow up* in the Lord and set a new standard for your life. I'm inviting you to choose a one-hundred-day season of faith that could be the most meaningful decision of your life.

A hundred days from now, you may look back on this moment and think, *That was the moment when things began to change.* Accept this invitation and notice how you begin to see the world in a different light. But don't just notice—take note. Use a journal to record how your spiritual habits are changing, the way your heart attitudes are shifting. Write about the rewards the Lord began to materialize in your life so that, when the darker days come, you will have a sort of memorial to remind yourself of God's faithfulness.

Make a note on your calendar of the day you started this walk and mark the days as you progress. Keep or carry around a copy of the ten expressions of faith with you as a reminder. If you feel like you are struggling in certain areas, go back to the corresponding chapters to be reminded of the benefits of choosing the Lord in that way.

If you feel your strength diminishing, use the prayers in the back of this book. God will sustain you—his strength is made perfect in your weakness. Write your own prayers in a journal and refer back to them, or say them aloud, as many times as it takes. Share the prayer with someone close to you and ask them to pray it with you. Perhaps you can recruit a friend to walk through these one hundred days with you, so you can pray for and encourage one another.

As you read the New Testament, following the reading plan in the back of this book, take notes in the margins of your Bible about the parts the Lord highlights for you. In time, as you revisit your notes, you will be amazed at the work that was being done in you through God's Word.

I can't promise this book will fix everything that ails you. But I do promise it is a doorway to a fuller, richer life of faith and spiritual connection. Will you take the first step through the door? Will you walk with me into new possibilities? If you make the commitment to establish real and lasting spiritual change in your life, you won't be disappointed.

Your life is of tremendous importance to God. The entire life of Jesus was an expression of God's concern for you. Your willing obedience to the truth is a powerful expression of love and gratitude for the Lord. When used together, these ten spiritual disciplines will help you experience God in every area of your life. Pursue these new life patterns with excitement and expectancy. God's Word never returns void. A life aligned with him will produce better outcomes.

AN EXERCISE OF INTENT

Though the idea of signing an agreement to commit to one hundred days of faith may seem silly, it's amazing how putting something in writing and signing on the line will help keep you focused on your pursuit. On the next page, you will find an agreement, to yourself, to commit to experiencing the good and abundant life that God intends for you to live. I invite you to read it, pray over it, and sign on the line.

A PRAYER FOR COMMITMENT

Heavenly Father, give me the strength to overcome the resistance of the enemy and to remain committed to you. Draw me closer to you that I may know you more and more every day. Help me to be more aware of your presence and strength than I am of those things that challenge me. Grant me rest and renewal as I turn my heart toward you. In Jesus' name, amen.

COMMITMENT TO ONE HUNDRED
DAYS OF INTENTIONAL FAITH

I, _____, understand that intending to follow God is evidenced by action. Over the course of one hundred days, I commit myself to expressing my intent through action; particularly, through the actions outlined in this book. Throughout these one hundred days of faith, I choose to align my life with the heart of God. I will focus on the following ten expressions of faith, and declare that from now on:

1. Intend to grow.
2. Intend to read the New Testament.
3. Intend to pray.
4. Intend to honor God in your home.
5. Intend to work with integrity.
6. Intend to teach the younger generation.
7. Intend to practice forgiveness.
8. Intend to welcome the Holy Spirit.
9. Intend to cultivate generosity.
10. Intend to finish well.

By signing below, I agree to finish the course God has marked out for my life, to stand firm on the name of Jesus, and to give my best in pursuit of him.

Signature: _____

Date: _____

Let's finish the course God has marked out for us. You will never regret giving your best in pursuit of God!

CONCLUSION

As we end, and you begin, I want to leave you with some encouragement.

One of my greatest assignments and passions is helping people become more fully devoted followers of Jesus Christ. Each week I stand up in front of the congregation and tell them they can be healed, restored, forgiven, and made new. The uncomfortable reality I live with is that I can't heal a gnat's wing, much less bring resolution to the deep-seated problems many of us face. But as I've walked through this life with others, I've gained an immovable confidence that no matter what life circumstance someone is facing, Jesus has an answer for them.

The Bible is full of almost unfathomable miracles initiated by practical obedience. In obedience, Moses raised his staff and the Red Sea parted. Through prayer, the dead were raised again to life and wholeness. With the help of the Holy Spirit and the knowledge of Scripture, Jesus silenced every temptation of the enemy. Over and over, the supernatural intervention of God is brought to bear on behalf of those willing to align their lives with the heart of God.

I want you to know that God, the Creator of heaven and earth, loves you deeply. He loves you right where you are, with everything you're carrying, and with all the failures that play on repeat in your head when the lights go out.

I pray the truth of God's love for you and pray his power to work on your behalf will be constant reminders that it's never too late to choose to move closer to him. Whether you've been following the Lord for decades, or you find yourself questioning the whole thing, you can draw nearer to the Lord—and he will draw nearer to you. God not only meets us where we are, but he stands on the edge of who we imagine ourselves to be. He is beckoning us out onto the water—out of our comforts and routines—and into a living faith, with benefits here on earth and for eternity.

The One you're serving is faithful and true. I pray you'll take this step. I know he will change the trajectory of your entire story.

NEW TESTAMENT READING PLAN FOR ONE HUNDRED DAYS

With about ten minutes a day and this reading plan, you have the exact scriptures you will need for each of your one hundred days to complete the New Testament. As you read, notice new ideas, new thoughts, and new strength begin to emerge, both while you read and throughout the day. It's worth the investment of ten minutes a day.

Tips and Best Practices

- If possible, schedule a time to read in the morning with your prayer time. When what's important to you gets put first, it gets done. Plus, this allows you to start your day off with the spiritual nourishment needed to give you a kingdom perspective as you go through your day.

- If you miss a day, don't be discouraged. If you need to give yourself a little leeway, or a couple of days off, read for twenty minutes for a couple of days ahead or afterward to catch up. Bottom line: don't give up. If you find yourself lagging far behind, just pick up where you left off and take it one day at a time.

- Make notes in your Bible as you read along. If you can't write in the Bible you have, invest in a new one that you can. It will become valuable as you use it as a life tool.

- If you find yourself struggling with lack of focus or comprehension, or if you suddenly become sleepy when reading, use the prayers in Appendix B, Section 2, to help get you through.

Reading Plan

Day 1: Matthew 1–2

Day 2: Matthew 3–4

Day 3: Matthew 5–6

Day 4: Matthew 7–8

Day 5: Matthew 9–10

Day 6: Matthew 11–12

Day 7: Matthew 13–14

Day 8: Matthew 15–17

Day 9: Matthew 18–19

Day 10: Matthew 20–21

Day 11: Matthew 22–23

Day 12: Matthew 24–25

Day 13: Matthew 26

Day 14: Matthew 27–28

Day 15: Mark 1–3

Day 16: Mark 4–5

Day 17: Mark 6–7

Day 18: Mark 8–9

Day 19: Mark 10–11

Day 20: Mark 12–14

Day 21: Mark 15–16

Day 22: Luke 1–3

Day 23: Luke 4–5

Day 24: Luke 6–7

Day 25: Luke 8–9

Day 26: Luke 10–11

Day 27: Luke 12–13

Day 28: Luke 14–16

Day 29: Luke 17–18

Day 30: Luke 19–20

Day 31: Luke 21–22

Day 32: Luke 23–24

Day 33: John 1–3

Day 34: John 4–7

Day 35: John 8–10

Day 36: John 11–13

Day 37: John 14–16

Day 38: John 17–19

Day 39: John 20–21

Day 40: Acts 1–2

Day 41: Acts 3–4

Day 42: Acts 5–6

Day 43: Acts 7–8

Day 44: Acts 9–10

Day 45: Acts 11–13

Day 46: Acts 14–15

Day 47: Acts 16–17

Day 48: Acts 18–20

Day 49: Acts 21–23

Day 50: Acts 24–26

Day 51: Acts 27–28

Day 52: Romans 1–2

Day 53: Romans 3–4

Day 54: Romans 5–7

Day 55: Romans 8–10

Day 56: Romans 11–13

Day 57: Romans 14–16

Day 58: 1 Corinthians 1–2

Day 59: 1 Corinthians 3–4

Day 60: 1 Corinthians 5–8

Day 61: 1 Corinthians 9–12

Day 62: 1 Corinthians 13–16

Day 63: 2 Corinthians 1–2

Day 64: 2 Corinthians 3–4

Day 65: 2 Corinthians 5–6

Day 66: 2 Corinthians 7–8

Day 67: 2 Corinthians 9–10

Day 68: 2 Corinthians 11–13

Day 69: Galatians 1–2

Day 70: Galatians 3–4

Day 71: Galatians 5–6

Day 72: Ephesians 1–3

Day 73: Ephesians 4–6

Day 74: Philippians 1–4

Day 75: Colossians 1–4

Day 76: 1 Thessalonians 1–5

Day 77: 2 Thessalonians 1–3

Day 78: 1 Timothy 1–6

Day 79: 2 Timothy 1–4

Day 80: Titus 1–3; Philemon 1

Day 81: Hebrews 1–3

Day 82: Hebrews 4–7

Day 83: Hebrews 8–10

Day 84: Hebrews 11–13

Day 85: James 1–5

Day 86: 1 Peter 1–5

Day 87: 2 Peter 1–3

Day 88: 1 John 1–5;
2 John 1

Day 89: 3 John 1

Day 90: Jude 1; Revelation
1–2

Day 91: Revelation 3–4

Day 92: Revelation 5–6

Day 93: Revelation 7–8

Day 94: Revelation 9–10

Day 95: Revelation 11–12

Day 96: Revelation 13–14

Day 97: Revelation 15–16

Day 98: Revelation 17–18

Day 99: Revelation 19–20

Day 100: Revelation 21–22

APPENDIX B

COLLECTION OF PRAYERS

1. Intend to Grow

Almighty God, I come to you in humility—I need your mercy. I cannot bring freedom and deliverance to myself. I lay aside my attempts and accept your provision for my life. Forgive me of my sin as I forgive those who sin against me. I choose to live so that Jesus may be honored through my life. I receive him as Lord of all that I am. I rejoice that in Christ I am free of guilt and shame. I am a child of the living God. May Jesus' name be praised. Amen.

Heavenly Father, I invite you to make me a person of character, courage, and boldness for your kingdom. I trust you with my life. In Jesus' name, amen.

Heavenly Father, I choose to serve you, to give you first place in my life. Help me to intentionally follow you daily.

Give me a willing spirit to grow, so I can fulfill the plans you have for me. In the name of Jesus, amen.

Heavenly Father, I come before you to declare my intent to grow up in you. May your truth be evident in my words and actions to myself and others. I welcome the Holy Spirit to guide me and convict me to stay the course you have ordained for me. Lord, I need your wisdom and direction every day. May all that I do be pleasing to you and increase my faith. In Jesus' name, amen.

Heavenly Father, it is easy to forget that you can do anything. There are no limits for you, except for boundaries created by my own unbelief. Help me to grow in faith so that I can see you doing the impossible in my generation. In Jesus' name, amen.

Heavenly Father, thank you for the examples of faith and courage you have given me in Scripture. Like those men and women of faith, make me a person of character, courage, and boldness for your kingdom. I put my trust in you, knowing that there is no fear in your perfect love. I choose to honor you all of my days. In Jesus' name, amen.

Heavenly Father, you are the truth—all truth comes from you. Grow in me a deeper understanding of your character and help me be a person of truth, modeling you in all I do.

Give me the diligence to put action to my desire to grow in you. May I lift your name so others will know and honor you. In Jesus' name, amen.

2. Intend to Read the New Testament

Almighty God, in you is found truth, life, and all things. My desire is to know you. Open my heart to your Word. Lead me in the pathway of life and fulfillment. My trust is in you, my God and my Redeemer. Amen.

Heavenly Father, as I read your Word, I pray it washes and renews my mind, bringing transformation. Help me seek you with greater intentionality. Protect me from any distractions or things that may confuse my understanding of your truth. I trust you to lead me toward maturity in Jesus Christ as I practice a daily relationship with you. In Jesus' name, amen.

Heavenly Father, I pray for understanding as I read your Word that I may comprehend the story. Give me clarity of your direction for my life through this purposeful time with you. Give me a hunger for your truth so that I pursue reading your Word with focused intention. I thank you for the Holy Spirit. I ask for his guidance as I peruse your truth. In Jesus' name, amen.

Heavenly Father, your faithfulness is infinite. As I read your Word, may the Holy Spirit teach me what I need to know for each season. Father, make your Word effective in my spirit and allow me to see and understand it afresh. I praise you for aligning my heart with yours through this time with you. In Jesus' name, amen.

Heavenly Father, open my mind to understand your Word, which reveals your character and your ways. I want to be more like you and choose to submit my heart and mind to you to transform them for useful service in your kingdom. As I read your Word, please highlight the things you want to impress upon my heart. In Jesus' name, amen.

Heavenly Father, teach me your ways. Help me not only to read your Word but to obey your instruction. I desire your truth in my heart. During this time with you, I pray you will grant me the strength to complete all for which you have created me. I pray for the ability to be alert and focused while reading your Word that I may grow to walk more fully in your light. In Jesus' name, amen.

3. Intend to Pray

Heavenly Father, teach me to come boldly to you in prayer with the help of the Holy Spirit. Help me to become increasingly at ease talking to and petitioning you—both privately and publicly—that many hearts and lives may be changed. In Jesus' name, amen.

Heavenly Father, I rejoice today in the joy of my salvation. Your Word brings light and life to me. The Holy Spirit directs my steps, illumines my mind, and reveals your wisdom. My hope is anchored in the victory of my Lord and Savior, Jesus of Nazareth. Throughout my days on this earth, may his name be exalted and his kingdom extended. Amen.

Heavenly Father, thank you for hearing my prayers and for the Holy Spirit, who teaches me how to pray. I am overwhelmed that you would want to have a personal conversation with me. Forgive me for taking this gift for granted. Protect me from any distractions that may interrupt my thoughts while in prayer. In Jesus' name, amen.

Heavenly Father, teach me to believe, to pray with faith, and to submit to your purposes. All things are possible with you. I humbly bring you issues that are beyond change without your intervention. Help me to persevere until you reveal your answers. Give me wisdom to ask for the right things and to trust in your timing. In Jesus' name, amen.

Heavenly Father, nothing is too hard for you. Teach me to intercede effectively. Help me to believe you will respond in great power to the needs I present—both privately and publicly. May your miraculous answers to prayer cultivate greater faith in you. In his name I pray, amen.

Heavenly Father, thank you for allowing and encouraging me to come boldly before you with my requests. I give my burdens and concerns about _____ to you. You are strong, loving, and faithful. All glory, honor, and praise belong to you. In Jesus' name, amen.

Heavenly Father, I ask the Holy Spirit to prompt me to bring things to you in prayer throughout my days. Teach me to pray, without ceasing, for your church and purposes around the world. I thank you that my time spent with you in prayer strengthens my ability to hear your voice and direction. In Jesus' name, amen.

4. Intend to Honor God in Your Home

Heavenly Father, I want to live a life that is pure before you, even when no one is watching. Help me to recognize anything that goes on behind closed doors of my home that is destructive to having a closer relationship with you, and give me the strength to leave those things behind. I pray that my life will bring honor and glory to you. In Jesus' name, amen.

Heavenly Father, I ask that you illuminate any way within me or in my home that is not aligned with your will. I ask the Holy Spirit to break through any darkness that may be standing in the way of your best for my life. I pray that I not just pretend you are Lord of my life in public, but that I completely submit to you in anything that may be hidden. Forgive me for my rebellion. Give me the strength to come into alignment with you concerning everything I do in private, every relationship in my home, every way I choose to spend my time. In Jesus' name, amen.

Heavenly Father, help me to see and release anything keeping me from your best that may not be known in public. I don't want to hold on to excuses or justify them. I want to honor you. I want your power to be released into my life. I want your freedom. Holy Spirit, fill me with God's grace, and help me be available to him. In Jesus' name, amen.

Heavenly Father, help me to recognize anything I do, say, or partake in that is coming between you and me in my private life. Give me the strength to lay down any bad habits that have dominated my home. Help me to set my private life into alignment with you, so that I may live in freedom. In Jesus' name, amen.

Heavenly Father, forgive me for the times I have not acted in a way that puts you first, with my family or in my home. I want to commit my time and resources to advance your kingdom, in public and in private. Direct my steps that my life would honor you alone. Show me any way within me that is preventing the power of your Spirit to work in my life. May the words of my mouth and the meditations of my heart be pleasing to you. In Jesus' name, amen.

5. Intend to Work with Integrity

Heavenly Father, help me to be a person of integrity and to value my work. I thank you for the strength to stand against discouragement. Help me to see the people I work with through your eyes. Thank you for entrusting me with the opportunity to serve you diligently and bear fruit for your kingdom in every environment you place me. In Jesus' name, amen.

Heavenly Father, help me to be grateful and not grumble. Teach me to guard my heart from attitudes that rob me of the peace and joy that come in serving you. Fill my heart with appreciation for my job and the purpose-filled life you intend me to live. I pray that I grow to work in such a way that it will be received by you as worship. In Jesus' name, amen.

Heavenly Father, thank you for the opportunities and relationships that I come across in my work to reflect your character. Give me the perspective and endurance to work in a way that brings honor to you and blessings to those around me. In Jesus' name, amen.

Heavenly Father, thank you for those who have modeled good work habits, teaching me the value of finishing a job, no matter how difficult. Thank you for giving me a sound mind and strength to work and diligently serve you all my days. In Jesus' name, amen.

Heavenly Father, thank you for the influence you have given me in every area of my life. Help me to keep in mind that I am working for you, wherever I am and whatever I am doing. I pray that others will see you through the way I conduct myself and in the quality of my work. Let me work to the fullest, to fulfill your will for my life. In Jesus' name, amen.

6. Intend to Teach the Younger Generation

Heavenly Father, I want the children in my sphere of influence to know you and to live for you. May they each have a personal experience with you and call upon Jesus as their

Savior and Lord. May they be able to trust you in the storms of life. In Jesus' name, amen.

Heavenly Father, thank you for the privilege of being your ambassador to the next generation. May my words and deeds represent you well. Thank you for inviting me to invest my strength and resources in pursuit of your agenda, bringing eternal value to my life and others. In Jesus' name, amen.

Heavenly Father, help me to be a reflection of you to the children within my influence, so that they will know your blessings as I do. Help me to be an example to them of obedient trust and truth and of dependence on you in every respect. In Jesus' name, amen.

Heavenly Father, help me to recognize any opportunities to reflect the love of Christ to the younger generation, especially to those who have never seen him nor felt his warmth. I am a thankful servant who is glad you sent someone to show me the light of Christ. Help me to go and do the same. In Jesus' name, amen.

7. Intend to Practice Forgiveness

Heavenly Father, thank you for forgiving me while I was yet a sinner and in rebellion toward you. I choose to forgive anyone for any and all offenses against me. I ask you to have mercy on my adversaries, blessing them by revealing your love and drawing them close to you. Today, I rejoice that your mercy endures forever. In Jesus' name, amen.

Heavenly Father, as you have forgiven me, I forgive anyone who has hurt or rejected me, releasing them from anything I think they owe me. Thank you for the salvation, deliverance, and restoration available through the cross of Jesus Christ. In his name, amen.

Heavenly Father, as you have graciously forgiven me, I also forgive _____ for their offense. Please bless them. I choose to cancel their debt to me right now, because you canceled mine when you forgave me. Thank you for setting me free. In Jesus' name, amen.

Heavenly Father, give me the perseverance to pursue you in adversity. I need your power to break the chains of unforgiveness and bitterness. The battle is first won in my mind and will. I choose, therefore, to forgive everyone of everything. In Jesus' name, amen.

8. Intend to Welcome the Holy Spirit

Heavenly Father, thank you for sending the Holy Spirit. I ask that you fill me with his presence. Give me an obedient and cooperative heart that I might clear away all ungodliness. Help me to have the discernment to know and embrace your ways. Please guide me toward a more abundant life in you. In Jesus' name, amen.

Heavenly Father, help me embrace the Holy Spirit every day, inviting him to guide my thoughts and actions. Teach me to regard your ways above my own. Turn me toward your perspective and away from unfruitful and limiting thoughts. I choose to submit to your Word and the Holy Spirit to transform me. In Jesus' name, amen.

Heavenly Father, thank you for the gift of the Holy Spirit. I invite him to be in my midst—guiding, convicting, and turning my heart toward honoring you. Help me to be increasingly committed to your kingdom and purposes. In Jesus' name, amen.

Heavenly Father, here I am. Prepare me to do my best for your kingdom. I want to see the Holy Spirit's power living in and through my life. When you invite me to do the impossible, help me to remember that it is in the impossible that I see your power living in me. I believe that when I am afraid, you will give me courage. I praise you for what you will do in my life. In Jesus' name, amen.

Heavenly Father, serving you is an entrusted privilege, and I need the help of the Holy Spirit to lead me and align my heart, attention, and words to your wisdom. Help me always to welcome and be filled to overflowing with the Holy Spirit. In Jesus' name, amen.

Heavenly Father, my times are in your hands, and your timing is perfect. Only by the Holy Spirit can I fulfill your assignments. Help me to keep in step with him, obedient not only in the "what" but also in the "when" and the "how." In Jesus' name, amen.

9. Intend to Cultivate Generosity

Heavenly Father, I choose to seek your perspective on money and all the things money can do. I pray for contentment with the blessings you have poured over my life. Give me a generous spirit in all things that I may reflect your generosity. Thank you for the promise that you will never leave me or forsake me, for that is worth more than all the world's riches. In Jesus' name, amen.

Heavenly Father, thank you for all the ways you bless me and the people around me, for all the big things we can see and all the small things you invite me to witness. Help me to remember that every good thing comes from you. Give me a heart of love and generosity toward others, so that I would be as eager to celebrate when you bless them as I am when you bless me. In Jesus' name, amen.

10. Intend to Finish Well

Heavenly Father, prepare me to endure through trials, and strengthen and equip me to honor you by helping others experiencing pain and suffering. As I focus on you, I trust that you will provide everything I would need for victory in each season of my life. Forgive me for any shortsighted self-interest that resists yielding to the Holy Spirit. In Jesus' name, amen.

Heavenly Father, teach me perseverance when I am tempted to give up. Sharpen my vision when I cannot see your path clearly and am tempted to go my own way. Give me strength to run my race with the end clearly in focus. And help me bring glory to you with every step I take. In Jesus' name, amen.

Heavenly Father, help me to stand in this season. I want to serve you with all that I am and with all that I have. I will strive to avoid evil at all costs. I will seek you and look for the opportunities you provide for me with a grateful heart. I will choose to be a light among my friends and acquaintances, so they can see that Jesus Christ is Lord over my life. In Jesus' name, amen.

Heavenly Father, I choose to walk out my circumstances with you. My situation may not be what I would prefer, but I wait in anticipation for the things I will learn through it. Help me to fix my eyes not on what is seen but on what is unseen. I thank you in advance for how we will walk through this season together. May my life be pleasing to you. In Jesus' name, amen.

Heavenly Father, prepare me to persevere through life's trials that I may receive the crown of life promised to those who stand faithful to your Word. Give me the strength of character like that of those in Scripture. Let the Holy Spirit bring me the necessary understanding to be faithful when the unexpected happens. I pray to finish well in every season, so that my life is a reflection of your faithfulness. In Jesus' name, amen.

Heavenly Father, I commit myself to your care, wisdom, and strength. My desire is to please and honor you all of my days. Give me the boldness and humility to follow you with joy and a steady, constant faith. Thank you for your great deliverance. I pray that you will enable me to stand firm for your purposes and never grow weary in doing good. In Jesus' name, amen.

Heavenly Father, give me a fresh filling of the kind of faith that David had. Faith that believes you can do anything and trusts you to make a difference in my life. May I never lose heart, Lord. Help me to depend on you as I face the big and small challenges before me. In Jesus' name, amen.

Heavenly Father, I choose Jesus as Lord of my life again today. Grant me the will to obey and serve you without reservation, and to choose your truth with the commitment to guard my heart against competitors. Thank you for your love and faithfulness in my life. I choose to honor you all of my days. In Jesus' name, amen.

Other Prayers

For Protection

Heavenly Father, I acknowledge you as Lord of my life. I praise you that, through the blood of Jesus, I have been redeemed from the hand of the devil. I praise you that the blood of Jesus continually cleanses me from all sin. Thank you that I am justified and made righteous, that I am sanctified, made holy, and set apart for your purposes. You are my refuge and my fortress. Thank you that you command your angels concerning me and they guard my life. In Jesus' name, amen.

Heavenly Father, I rejoice in the protection of an Almighty God—my shield and my strength. Your grace and mercy sustain me. The Holy Spirit is my Helper. Through Jesus' blood, I am delivered out of the hand of the enemy and held secure in the hand of my Creator. My hope is anchored in the faithfulness of my Lord and Redeemer. In Jesus' name, amen.

Heavenly Father, I thank you for your protection over my mind, body, and spirit. I thank you that, through the blood of Jesus, I have been given authority over any and all dark spiritual forces. I thank you that the darkness yields as I speak the name of Jesus. I praise you for your rescue. In Jesus' name, amen.

Against Worry, Fear, and Anxiety

Heavenly Father, nothing is hidden from you. I know you are aware of my fears. Today, I choose to lay them down before you. Help me to trust in your greater plan and be confident that you are directing all things for my good. Open my heart to see fear and anxiety as an unwelcome intruder that has been defeated through the cross and has no power over me. Help me to depend on you through the battles that life presents. Help me to take captive every thought to make it obedient to your truth for my life. I choose to fully receive the peace that you have given freely. In Jesus' name, amen.

Heavenly Father, thank you that in this troubled world you provide peace, security, and abundant life through the cross of Jesus Christ. May the Holy Spirit counsel me daily in your peace. When I am afraid, I will trust in you. In Jesus' name, amen.

Heavenly Father, when I am tempted to worry, may the Holy Spirit help me to recognize it as sin and confess it to you. Help me to transfer my trust to you from anyone or anything other than you. You alone are my source and security. In Jesus' name, amen.

Heavenly Father, I believe all good things originate from you. When life feels out of control, I choose to yield to you and trust that you are working out your purposes. I will not fear rejection from others. And instead of worrying, I will keep walking in obedience to your Word, doing the best I know to do and trusting in the Holy Spirit. In Jesus' name, amen.

Heavenly Father, I am grateful for your plans and provisions, and I trust your watchful care over my life. When I am afraid I will not have enough, remind me of your generosity. When I am tempted to be anxious about my circumstances, give me a spirit of peaceful contentment. I will trust in you, my Lord and my Redeemer. In Jesus' name, amen.

Heavenly Father, often my life looks and feels like a crisis in motion. Those are the times I need you the most. Please forgive me when I fall into worry, and my emotions give way to stress. Strengthen me to give you my best, both in and out of my comfort zones. In Jesus' name, amen.

Heavenly Father, in this sinful world with dark forces, you are a shelter for the oppressed, a refuge in times of trouble. Forgive me when I have succumbed to fear and not cried out to you for rescue. Thank you for your unfailing promise of protection. In Jesus' name, amen.

Heavenly Father, I am buffeted by a rapidly changing world and ever increasing demands. I am often fearful, off-balance, and even angry. Help me to remember that you are my foundation and my strength. When I am weak, your strength is sufficient. When my faith is small, you are faithful. Keep my path clearly marked, so that I will always honor you. In Jesus' name, amen.

Heavenly Father, forgive me when fear throttles my trust in you. No thing and no one can separate me from you. Because of you, I will not fear what man can do to me. I am yours. I am not my own. I have been bought with a price, the blood of Jesus. In his name, amen.

Against Depression

Heavenly Father, I ask that you deliver me from the spirit of heaviness. I trust that you work all things together for my good. Help me to take every thought captive and make it obedient to the truth of what your Word says the blood of Jesus has done for me. Fill me with joy and peace. I ask that you renew my mind and strength through the power of the Holy Spirit. In Jesus' name, amen.

Heavenly Father, I ask for your protection in the battlefield of my mind. Give me the strength to open my mouth in praise when I am feeling attacked. Still my anxiousness with your peace. Through the blood of Jesus, I have been delivered out of the hand of the enemy. My life is secure in the hand of my Creator. In Jesus' name, amen.

Heavenly Father, I claim Jesus as Lord of my life. Today, I lay aside the spirit of heaviness and raise my voice in praise of the Lord, my strength and my redeemer. My hope is in you, and I trust you with my life. In Jesus' name, amen.

Against Temptation

Heavenly Father, when I face temptation, I will fear no evil, for I know you are with me. Give me the wisdom to do all I can to avoid the places that are designed to separate me from your best. Help me to keep my eyes on Christ, my Savior. In Jesus' name, amen.

Heavenly Father, temptations present themselves. But through the cross, your kingdom is within me, and I am rescued from darkness—forgiven and reconciled to you. Thank you for your merciful provision that purchased my victory over evil. In Jesus' name, amen.

Heavenly Father, seeking your will is a priority. May temptations and distractions never weaken my commitment and devotion to you or accomplish the enemy's plan to take me off course. May your name be honored through my choices. In Jesus' name, amen.

Heavenly Father, whatever temptations to sin come my way, help me to quickly seek out and cooperate with your Word. Thank you for the Holy Spirit, who gives me discernment to know your voice and not be fooled by the deceptions of evil. In Jesus' name, amen.

Against Rejection

Heavenly Father, I declare Jesus as Lord. I thank you that, through the blood of Jesus Christ on the cross, the spirit of rejection has no authority over me and no rights to my life. Thank you that your Son endured all rejection on the cross so that it is defeated in my life. I choose now to forgive anyone and everyone who has rejected me. Lord, draw them into you and bless them. I receive your freedom from rejection now. Give me a revelation of your love and acceptance of me. In Jesus' name, amen.

Heavenly Father, as you have forgiven me, I forgive anyone who has hurt or rejected me. I release them from anything I think they owe me. Thank you for the salvation, deliverance, and restoration available through the cross of Jesus Christ. In his name, amen.

Heavenly Father, I confidently come to you through the cross, where your sinless Son endured rejection, abandonment, shame, and guilt so that I could be free. I choose to forgive those who have rejected or harmed me. Today, I will rejoice in your great love and in the victory Jesus of Nazareth won for me through his death and resurrection. In Jesus' name, amen.

For Healing

Heavenly Father, thank you for your restoration and healing. You bring possibility to the impossible. Help me to remember this when everything seems hopeless, and to fearlessly invite you to make a difference in hard circumstances. In Jesus' name, amen.

Heavenly Father, I acknowledge all your benefits. Through the cross, I have complete forgiveness for my sins and healing from all diseases. You have redeemed my life from destruction. You have crowned me with love and compassion. And you satisfy my life with good things. Thank you for all the ways you enrich my days. In Jesus' name, amen.

Heavenly Father, you are worthy of all my praise in times of both ease and difficulty. I praise you for the cross and all you have provided—salvation, deliverance, and healing. May my words reflect the praise in my heart so others will see you in my life. In Jesus' name, amen.

Heavenly Father, I lift up to you those in my life who need your healing and whose hearts are hopeless and broken. I have seen you restore my hope and give purpose back to my life. Help me to share what you have done for me with those who suffer. In Jesus' name, amen.

Heavenly Father, I thank you that you are healing my mind, my body, and my spirit. I ask for your restoration. I invite the Holy Spirit to direct me in how to walk in your healing. In Jesus' name, amen.

For Freedom from Addiction

Heavenly Father, I ask for your strength in fighting against the spirit of addiction. In the name of Jesus, no form of darkness has authority over me or permission to control me. Lord, I thank you that you know the plans you have for me, plans of good and not of evil, plans of prosperity and not of calamity, and plans to give me a future and a hope. In Jesus' name, amen.

Heavenly Father, I thank you that you have the ability to pull down strongholds in my life. Help me to stand against any temptation that may try to draw me into darkness. Give me the strength to lay down anything that opposes your plans for my life. In Jesus' name, amen.

Heavenly Father, I thank you that my life has been redeemed through the blood of Jesus. I ask that the power of the Holy

Spirit help me to break free from any dark spiritual forces that may be battling for control over my life. I claim Jesus as Lord of my life, and I choose to walk in your freedom. In Jesus' name, amen.

ACKNOWLEDGMENTS

My life is captured in the image of a turtle on a fence post: it is obvious someone has helped with the destination. God has provided a series of voices and mentors to help shape the ideas that are shared in this book. Without their coaching and encouragement, I would be a very different man. Derek Prince, Dr. Howard Ervin, Sir Lionel Luckhoo, and Aunt Mary were all strategically placed along my journey. My parents modeled a faith that could not be ignored. My brothers have walked the journey with me. My wife has patiently endured my stumbling efforts to learn and grow in faith. To God be the glory.

NOTES

Chapter 8: Intend to Work with Integrity

1. Deloitte, "The Deloitte Millennial Survey 2018," 27, https://www2.deloitte.com/content/dam/Deloitte/ch /Documents/human-capital/ch-2018-millennial-survey -global-report.pdf (accessed September 12, 2019).
2. "Deloitte Millennial Survey 2018," 17.
3. "Udemy in Depth: 2018 Workplace Distraction Report," February 2018, Udemy for Business, https://research.udemy .com/research_report/udemy-depth-2018-workplace -distraction-report.

Chapter 10: Intend to Practice Forgiveness

1. "Forgiveness: Your Health Depends on It," Johns Hopkins Medicine, https://www.hopkinsmedicine.org/health/wellness -and-prevention/forgiveness-your-health-depends-on-it (accessed August 16, 2019).
2. "Forgiveness," Johns Hopkins Medicine.
3. "Forgiveness," Johns Hopkins Medicine.

Chapter 12: Intend to Cultivate Generosity

1. Fara Warner, "Curb Your Enthusiasm," *Fast Company*, January 2002, https://www.fastcompany.com/44379/curb-your-enthusiasm.

2. *O Brother, Where Art Thou?* written, produced, and directed by Joel and Ethan Cohen, Touchstone Pictures, 2000.

Chapter 13: Intend to Finish Well

1. Kevin McSpadden, "You Now Have a Shorter Attention Span Than a Goldfish," *Time*, May 14, 2015, http://time.com/3858309/attention-spans-goldfish/.

ABOUT THE AUTHOR

Allen Jackson is passionate about helping people become more fully devoted followers of Jesus Christ who respond to God's invitations for their lives.

He has served World Outreach Church since 1981, becoming senior pastor in 1989. Under his leadership, WOC has grown to a congregation of over fifteen thousand people through outreach activities, community events, and worship services designed to share the gospel.

Through Allen Jackson Ministries, his messages reach people across the globe through television, radio, Sirius XM, and online streaming. His teachings are also available in published books and other resources.

With degrees from Oral Roberts University and Vanderbilt University, and additional studies at Gordon-Conwell Theological Seminary and Hebrew University of Jerusalem, Pastor Jackson is uniquely equipped to help people develop a love and understanding of God's Word.

Pastor Jackson's wife, Kathy, is an active participant in the ministry at World Outreach Church.